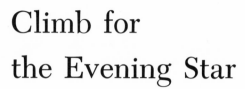

Climb for
the Evening Star

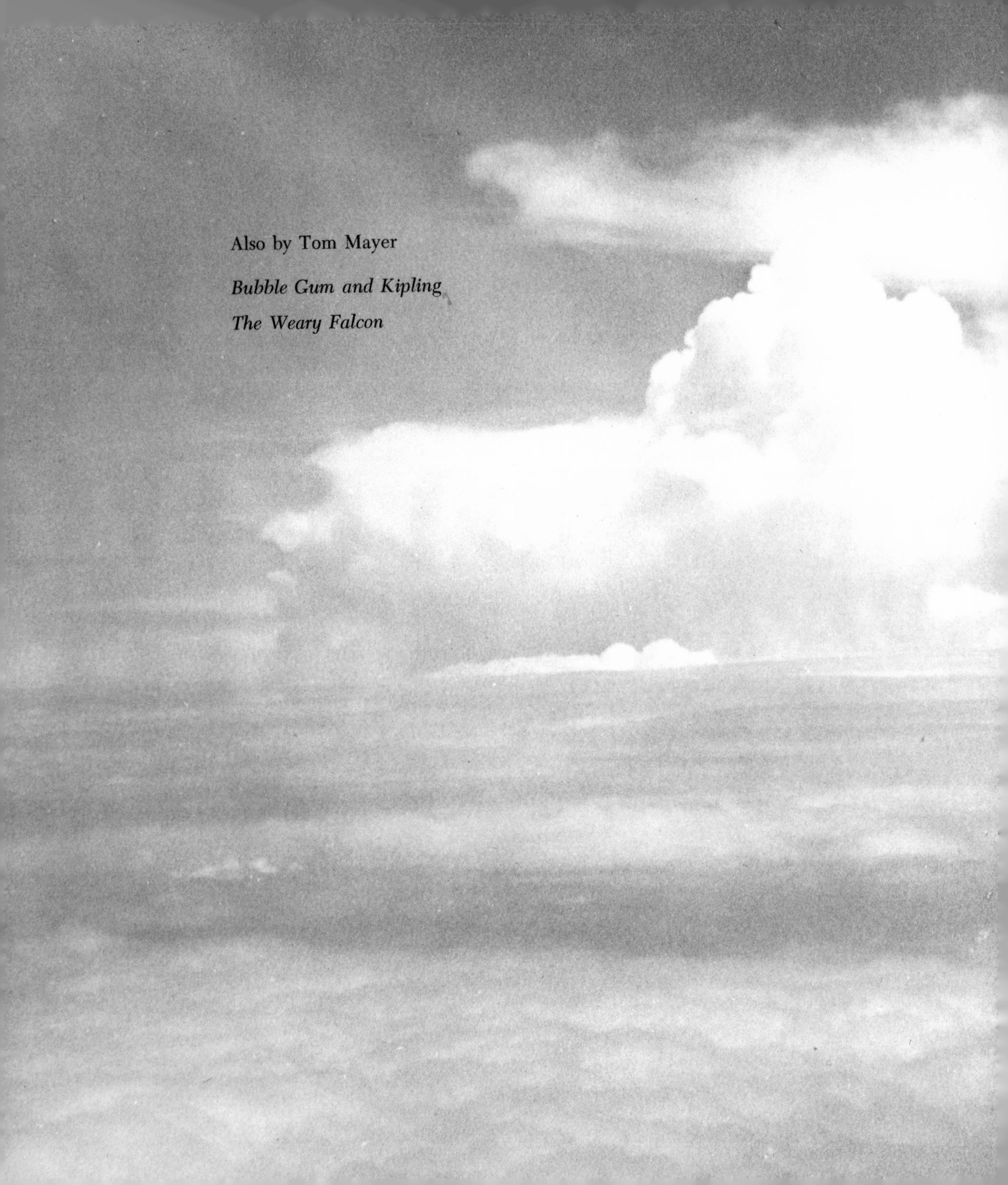

Also by Tom Mayer

Bubble Gum and Kipling

The Weary Falcon

Tom Mayer

Climb for the Evening Star

Houghton Mifflin Company Boston : 1974

First Printing   v

"An Irish Airman Foresees His Death" is reprinted with permission of Macmillan Publishing Co., Inc., from *Collected Poems* by William Butler Yeats. Copyright 1919 by Macmillan Publishing Co., Inc., renewed 1947 by Bertha Georgie Yeats.
Portions of this book have appeared in slightly different form in *Playboy* and *True Magazine*.

Cloud photographs by Freelance Photographers Guild, Inc.

Library of Congress Cataloging in Publication Data
Mayer, Tom.
  Climb for the evening star.
  1. Mayer, Tom. 2. Air pilots—Correspondence, reminiscences, etc. I. Title.
TL540.M373A33   629.13'092'4 B   73-21811
ISBN 0-395-18483-5

Printed in the United States of America

For Susan

In developing aviation, in making it a form of commerce, in replacing the wild freedom of danger with the civilized bonds of safety, must we give up this miracle of the air? Will men fly through the sky in the future without seeing what I have seen, without feeling what I have felt? Is that true of all things we call human progress — do the gods retire as commerce and science advance?

—CHARLES A. LINDBERGH
The Spirit of St. Louis

Climb for
the Evening Star

1

Sooner or later, if you are a pilot, almost everyone you know will ask you why you do it. The query usually comes in a rather avid, not altogether politely curious tone, a little like asking a nice girl how she ever got started, or a man why he's homosexual, or what it feels like to be black, as if the speaker expects an insight into a way of life so strange any true commentary must take the form of titillating revelation.

In proper spirit I reply, "It's like opium. Just as addictive and a lot more expensive." Or, "It saves a helluva psychiatrist's bill and it's much more fun." Flip answers to a heavy question, but not without an element of truth.

I learned to fly six years ago from a small and none too sterling outfit in San Antonio, Texas — the proprietor crashed the company's best charter plane into a graveyard the day before I started — and have not spent thirty consecutive days on the ground since. A long spell earthbound, anything more than a week, and I begin to suffer from a most unpleasant malaise not unlike withdrawal. I snap at friends, am incapable of work, feel as though I've just contracted the latest foreign flu. My wife, who from a keen sense of self-preservation has learned to detect the symptoms early, will say, "You need to get your rocks off. Go make it with your airplane."

And I say, "But I haven't got a trip. There's no reason to."

"Just take it up and do a few rolls. Then do a Cuban eight. Cuban eights always make you feel better."

"The FAA might catch me." The FAA is the Federal Aviation Administration, government watchdog of the sky. It takes a very dim view of unauthorized aerobatics.

"No they won't. They never have before. Do what I tell you. I know you'll feel better."

And off I go to the airport to commune with my airplane, a machine personified in my mind's eye as the big yellow bird, or the bitch, depending on the state of her mechanical health. Sick or healthy, she is never far from center stage in my life.

Officially she is a Beechcraft Model D–17S, a cabin biplane with retractable landing gear and negative stagger (that means the top wing is behind the bottom). Power, one Pratt and Whitney radial, 985 cubic inches displacement, capable of 450 horsepower. A direct descendant of engines made famous in the long ago by men like Wiley Post (who first charted jet streams and had only one eye), and Roscoe Turner (who carried a pet lion as a copilot). Popularly she is called a Staggerwing. Technically she belongs to aviation's Bronze Age. The prototype of her genre first

2

flew in 1932. Her wings are made of wood, spars like railroad ties breathed on by a master cabinetmaker, ribs that look like spruce miniatures of the Golden Gate Bridge. Her rudder post is a squared off telephone pole. She is covered with fabric, painted with many coats of dope that I spend a lot of time trying to keep polished to a high gloss. Her interior is spacious and handsomely upholstered. She carries four in great luxury, five in tourist-class comfort, and one time in Mexico we had nine in her. Practically . . . to fly her is to love her.

First, she is quite beautiful. Her wings end in graceful ellipses, like those of a Battle of Britain Spitfire, and her fuselage behind the cabin tapers down to a waist like a Vargas girl. The windshield slants rakishly. Her engine, nine cylinders arranged in a circle, each one bigger than an entire Volkswagen motor, is a glorious maze of chrome pushrod covers and ignition harness and cooling fins and breather ducting, and her spinner and prop, a giant scythe of a Hamilton Standard, glitter more brightly than all the diamonds in Cartier's. She is nostalgia unlimited and an object lesson in pure efficiency.

I climb in, twist through a labyrinth of monkey-bar size cabin bracings to the left seat. The pilot who checked me out on the plane said, "Getting in is the hard part. If you don't give yourself a concussion the worst is over." I fasten the belt, watch happily as my hands go about the half dozen tasks necessary to bring the Pratt to life. I think of my old flight instructor, a Baptist missionary who flew every kind of plane from J–3 Cubs to KC–135 tankers with the same inimitable tender elegance. He once said to me, "Starting modern opposed engines is easy. Starting turbines is so easy it's boring. But firing up a radial is like building a house. You get a real sense of accomplishment when you finish."

Fuel valve on center main. Mixture rich. Throttle cracked. Hit the

3

wobble pump for five pounds of fuel pressure. Work the primer, a cantankerous device for getting gas to the cylinders that on a cold morning would reduce Charles Atlas to frustrated tears. Magnetos hot. Battery switch on. With one hand press the starter button. With the other work the wobble pump again. With the other jiggle the throttle. With the other be ready to prime again.

Sometimes nothing happens. Once I was going to give an FAA man a ride, impress him and by proxy the rest of the federal government with the incomparable splendors of old airplanes and my flawless piloting technique. The prop wouldn't even turn over. Walter Beech, hoary progenitor of the strain, knew a lot about aerodynamics, had an eye for form da Vinci would have envied, but he studied the discoveries of Thomas Edison only casually. Battalions of mechanics and not a few engineers have wrestled futilely and expensively with the idiosyncracies of my Staggerwing's electrical system.

When she does go it's like dawn on an English airfield in every good-bad World War II movie ever made. A strained, utterly distinctive whine, a few prop blades flash, a pop like a twelve gauge shotgun, another, great farts of blue black smoke, the prop blurs, and she is running, a thundering grumble that is at once very loud and slightly irregular and gentle, a little like the purring of the biggest meanest lion who ever lived amplified a thousand times.

In the cockpit I am transformed. A friend, who is something of an old airplane nut himself, says, "I like to fly the Staggerwing with you. You grin like a horny Marine in a whorehouse all the time." It's true, probably. I no longer feel like Tom Mayer, itinerant writer and nine-to-five man in the University of New Mexico English Department. I am at the controls of a piece of history, the flagship of an era, the living emblem of a better,

4

freer, hopeful time. Who knows which famous ghosts ride my copilot's seat?

But at least a corner of my mind is all technician, absorbed by the timeless realities of oil pressure and cylinder head temperatures, radiator door settings and prop cycle and magneto drops. A Staggerwing is no docile museum piece, and I have great respect for her demands. In her heart, she makes few concessions to more modern planes. She is a big fast ship by any standards, everything about her designed for performance, honest enough if your hand is sure and firm, but no toy for children or weekend duffers.

Like all old timers she rests nose high — a taildragger in the vernacular — and her taxi visibility is nil. During groundhandling I remember the pilot — an excellent pilot, too, with more hours aloft than I have alive — who made kindling wood of a sawhorse while taxiing in a plane somewhat like her. The Pratt is one of the most trustworthy instruments ever devised, but any engine needs fuel. The Staggerwing has seven tanks, enough to keep her airborne nearly eight hours, but her plumbing is as complicated as the New York City subway system, and the pilot had best know it as well as the slant of his own handwriting or disaster will surely ensue. During approaches I remember the words of a student I was trying to teach to land another tail-wheel plane. They apply to the whole breed. "On the ground this thing has all the stability of Ralph Nader's Corvair with one rear tire blown out on an icy freeway at rush hour."

Since this is still 1972 I must also contend with the FAA, that bureaucratic handmaiden of science and commerce, and other planes. Alternator on. Radio on. Earphones on. Transponder to standby. Key the microphone. My best John Wayne voice. (My wife calls it my Captain America accent, giggles uncontrollably whenever she hears me on the airways.) "Santa Fe

5

Tower. Stagger Beech November six seven five four three, north hangars, taxi takeoff." From a half mile away, from behind a wall of inch-thick, green-tinted plate glass, comes the cool bored reply. "Five four three, runway two zero, wind calm, altimeter . . ."

Takeoff in the old girl is the essence of exhilaration. Line up on the center stripes, lock the tail wheel, quick last scan of the engine instruments to make sure the needles are all cradled in the green arcs. Long breath accompanied by the inevitable quickening of pulse. Throttle to the fire wall. The lion grumble swells to an earth-trembling, gut-deep roar, a note of pure power — no anemic opposed-engine buzz here — and we accelerate down the runway quickly, very quickly indeed, a yellow bolt launched from yesterday's crossbow. The tail comes up, an instant later the main wheels break ground and we are climbing. The whole process takes less than the length of two football fields (about half the distance most comparable new planes need), for Staggerwings were conceived in the days when any cow pasture was an airport. It is a trait I have been thankful for more than once in the 1970s.

I flip the gear switch to retract position and commence my final earth-connected act. The first Staggerwings had fixed gear, but in the interests of economy and speed the Beech Aircraft Company hired Rube Goldberg to redesign all three wheels so that they would tuck into the plane's belly in flight. The result was a characteristic contraption of bicycle chains and sprockets and large rubber bands called bungee cords actuated by an electric motor of feeble potency and dubious reliability. To help matters along I grab hold of a big wood-knobbed crank, ostensibly for emergencies only, and twist with the vigor of a sailor weighing a heavy anchor.

After considerable grunting and churning, a red light blinks on, tells me the wheels are up and locked. The bird is clean, running free in her element, easy as a shark in the open ocean. She climbs like the proverbial stripe-assed ape. We have two hundred feet passing the control tower, nearly a thousand by the end of the runway if we feel like it. Not a ship on the field can do better, including the turbo prop Convairs that belong to Frontier and Texas International.

We turn left, still climbing steeply, head for an area against the high peaks of the Sangre de Cristo Mountains where we will be unlikely to meet other planes, away from the prying eyes of the Feds. I do my best to scan every corner of the sky thoroughly. Santa Fe is not a busy field, but the specter of mid-air collision is never far from the surface of my mind near any terminal. In spite of sheafs of rules, perfect visibility, and radar, I have almost been picked off three times.

Once, practicing aerobatics in a designated area near Washington, D.C., I rolled level on top of an Immelmann and found myself eyeball to eyeball with a 727. We both broke into turns so steep I bet the airline had to deal with a small encyclopedia of passenger complaints. I had nightmares for a month. Another time was east of Las Vegas, New Mexico, a town with somewhat less air traffic than an average county seat in Outer Mongolia. I was in the Staggerwing, flying straight and level at a government-pre-scribed altitude, when a Cherokee Six, an ungainly aerial stationwagon by Piper, nearly chewed through my right top wing. In order to catch the yellow bird he must have been descending in a near terminal velocity dive. He never even saw us, leveled out, and when we overtook him he complained on the radio that our proximity was scaring his passengers. And a few months ago on this same field a Lear Jet misunderstood a command from the tower, took off when he was supposed to hold. I was departing on another runway and we came within death's eyelash of meeting at the intersection.

Fewer than five minutes have passed since we started our takeoff roll,

7

and we are three thousand feet above the New Mexico terrain. You can see seventy-five miles in any direction. The sky is a great inverted bowl of cold deep blue, unblemished except for the white plumes of several jet contrails to the south.

We do a couple of steep turns, exercises that enable us to feel each other out at the same time we make sure there are no other planes around. All clear. Pull the seat belt up another notch. Here we go. Nose down slightly for speed. Now bring the nose up and twist the wheel to the right and step on the rudder and the horizon spins, a marvelous kaleidoscope of sky and mountain and sun dazzle, and we are level again and still have plenty of speed and bring the nose up and around we go the other way. The old girl was born to roll, has very good fast ailerons. I open a side window just a crack to hear the symphony in the flying wires. Nose down for speed again and then back firmly on the wheel and the big yellow bird rockets past vertical with the wind in her wires like a flock of banshees and the mountain horizon hangs in front of us but the peaks are all upside down, point toward my feet. I let the nose cleave through them and we are rushing downhill accelerating incredibly on the backside of a loop.

For perhaps thirty minutes we make the earth and sky whirl and cavort, disappear and reappear in a variety of mad perspectives. We do a gentle and simple series of primary aerobatics: loops, barrel rolls, chandelles, modified point rolls, a couple of Cubans. The old girl ballerinas through them with never an indication of stress or strain or protest; the ancient wings pirouette, the bright spinner describes a lazy freehand on the sky, the big Pratt bellows and howls with delight in exercise. The yellow bird is as graceful and precise as Peggy Fleming or Anna Pavlova on the best days of their lives.

And me? I sit there in a state I can only describe as perfect contentment.

8

My hands and feet do what they must with the assurance of much practice, my eyes monitor instruments and judge heights and distances, but it is all so easy. There is plenty of time to savor each sensation and to think as well. It is peaceful up here. No intrusions, no telephones, no students, no typewriter, just sky and airplane and wind. Time and space, those frameworks of sorrow and frustration, are suspended, altered, fractured, infinitely variable, completely controllable. Who could help but be happy?

I remember a man with the unlikely name of Force O'Rear Treadaway, of Uvalde, Texas. Easy moving, erect, silvery, as at home in the air as an old albatross. Nothing could surprise him, or frighten him, for he had seen everything before, not once but many times. He had the tempered dignity of a good judge, was in fact empowered by the government to pass on my qualifications for a commercial pilot's license.

We were flying a tiny Cessna trainer in the bumpy sky north of Del Rio on my check ride a few days after Robert Kennedy had been shot in Los Angeles. It was an uncomfortable time to be in Texas. My liberal friends were agonized with the exhumation of old tragedy; an oil man said, "Well, at least they can't blame us this time"; a mechanic I met summarized redneck reaction: "Great. Only one more to go." The event and its ramifications were far from no one's mind, a cocklebur in the collective conscience, but Treadaway and I seemed bent on business as usual.

He asked me to do a lazy eight, a maneuver which properly executed requires very delicate control through a wide range of airspeeds and attitudes and should be one of the most graceful and soothing things you can do in an airplane. It was the only test item we had not covered. As the saying goes, I felt victory within my grasp, but knew the lazy eight to be a difficult and important maneuver, one examiners set great

9

store by, for it separates the pilots from the automatons. I had been practicing hard and ran one off with what I thought was reasonable competence.

"Here," Treadaway said. "Let me try one."

"What did I do wrong?" I saw months of work wasted, felt an exquisite humiliation. For an examiner to take the controls usually means failure.

"Nothing."

He did several with a fluidity I could never hope to match, an expression of rapt attention on his face that I would now suspect to be a mature version of my own whorehouse grin.

"You do one."

We alternated through several more, then started back to the field. I was sure I had failed, wondered how I could explain to my instructor, my friends, myself.

"You did fine," Treadaway said. "But I like to fly, too."

We bumped along awhile. I was puzzled, still very apprehensive. Treadaway took off his sunglasses and rubbed his eyes, smiled at me gravely.

"You know," he said, "If everybody knew how to fly, what happened in Los Angeles would never have happened."

So I got my commercial ticket and for years would amuse friends with my story of the philosopher-flight-examiner from Uvalde. Secretly I have always known him to be the wisest of men.

Finally it is time to come down. One last loop and the big yellow bird points her nose earthward. The airspeed needle slides smoothly around the dial to cover 230 mph, which for any light plane is hauling ass. A Staggerwing could outrun all but the hottest racing ships of her day. Turn up the radio volume. Voice from the tower rudely in my ear, "Enter left base two zero."

10

Helped by gravity the landing gear cranks down electrically, with much clattering of chains and wind buffeting, the bird's mild protest at returning to an environment she will never consider home. We touch, taxi to the hangar. I shut down the engine. The gyroscopic instruments make a friendly lingering whine. Everything appears different, sharper, fresher, newer, the world after a short afternoon rain. I make sure the Staggerwing is bedded comfortably, drive off in my car, but its controls feel puny and inexact, wrong. A part of me is still in the sky. I am tired, but it is the fatigue of a good massage rather than a day at the office. My mind is as clear as it will ever be. If someone asked me now why I fly, I could explain at least in part — there is the power and the quaint quirky romance, but most of all it is a way to tranquillity.

2

Forty-five minutes of play provide answers, but they are not the only ones. Lindbergh spoke of the "miracle of the air," and it is true, sometimes you do see things so beautiful, so extraordinary, so magical and profound that they may be described only in terms of the mystical. Such encounters invariably leave you changed; not made better or wiser, a safer pilot, more tactful, healthier or less an insomniac; no, the effects are in the realm of consciousness expansion.

Take a trip in central Mexico, a flight from the town of San Miguel de Allende to the metropolis of Guadalajara. It has been raining steadily for a week. The field at San Miguel, never more than a minimal sod strip, has been reduced to a near bog. The mountains — central Mexico is full of mountains, all shapes and sizes, which on occasion make for interesting problems in navigation — are invisible, packed in great wads of dirty cotton batting.

The time is break of dawn, and the countryside is awash with fog and hush. It is too wet for roosters, too early for people, cold enough for warm jackets. The grass squishes underfoot as I do my walk around, check fuel tanks for water contamination, add a gallon of oil, pull the prop through by hand to make sure none of the bottom cylinders have filled with oil, spray silicone lubricant on the gear slide tubes, wipe the layer of rainy oil from the windshield.

My two passengers, wife and brother-in-law, untie the ropes that hold the wings and tail to earth in case of strong winds. My wife is barely awake and shivering. My brother-in-law, the mad midget, white-haired, twelve going on eighty-seven, a personality perpetually ricocheting between Einsteinian gravity and Dennis the Menace, is playing the good copilot.

"All untied. We going on instruments?"

"We'll have to," I say. The ceiling is maybe two hundred feet.

"Good," my wife says. "I like clouds. It's all gray and cozy and introverted inside them."

We stow baggage, belt in, fire up. I taxi cautiously, head out the side window in the maelstrom of the prop blast for better view. Douglas does the same from the copilot's seat, hair streaming like some albino Indian chief on a war charge, a hand clasping his professorial horn rims. I know this field well, have been flying from it since I was in aeronautical swaddling clothes, which does not keep me from getting stuck with some regularity. Once I taxied the big yellow bird into muck up to her knees and it took five men, a tractor, and a mule to extract her. Had the same thing happened to a modern tri-gear the damage would have run into thousands of dollars, instead of just gallons of sweat.

14

At the east end of the runway I turn around, lock the tail wheel, run through my check list. The strip is on a hilltop, which creates some interesting optical effects. The runway is much foreshortened, like a slope photographed through a long lens. The windsock is over the brow. Though actually mounted on a twenty-foot pole, it looks from here as if it were pegged to the horizon. The already acute angle at which the Beech crouches is exaggerated by the rise, makes us feel as if we were in a rocket poised for nearly vertical launch. There is a cow off to the left, and I hope she has enough sense to stay there. I pull the carburetor heat on, and the engine rpms increase which means ice has been forming. Douglas notices, points.

"You got to watch it on mornings like this," I say. "Everybody belted in good?"

Carb heat to cold, throttle forward. We begin to trundle through the grass, very slowly at first, as the Pratt fights the grade and soft footing. We pass the cow, who raises her head solemnly to watch our progress. The tail comes up. The windsock pole appears like a periscope breaking water. The wheels unstick and I give the big yellow bird a mental pat on the back. She has used barely a thousand feet, even under these conditions. San Miguel is a true high-country bush field, well over a mile above sea level, less than a half mile long, and the air here never offers much substance to wings or prop. I think of a good dozen newer craft I have watched run along this grass to the last inch and stagger into the air graceless as a drunk. We have eighty miles an hour indicated passing the sock.

"Gear up," I say.

"Rog," says Douglas, and flips the switch for me.

I do my winching act, am applauded by the red light. I have held the bird low, not wanting to go on instruments in the midst of violent

15

exercise. Dead ahead lies the town, and we thunder down the main street still at full power and windmill height. I laugh thinking of the rattling windows and sleepy cursing tourists. For some reason it is only Americans who object to my machine, my low flying and impromptu air shows; I can walk nowhere in the town without at least a few small boys following me shouting in Spanish, "Tomás, Tomás, when will you take us for a ride? When will you loop the loop again?"

Rpms to 2000, cruise climb. Thirty inches of manifold pressure. I trim the nose upward a few degrees and the rate of climb needle crouches, then leaps. The prop hacks into an underbelly of mist. I wriggle deeper into the seat, settle on the gauges, adapt myself to a milieu where the senses are reduced to a role of pure treachery. An instant on the engine instruments — oil pressure, oil temperature, fuel pressure, cylinder heads, suction; an instant on the flight instruments — wings of the toy airplane in the gyro horizon steady, altimeter winding up, airspeed 115, gyro compass steady and it agrees with the magnetic compass. My right hand reaches over my shoulder, turns the rudder trim on the roof counterclockwise to help control the torque and asymmetrical propeller thrust. Engine instruments, flight instruments, my glance swings back and forth regular as the pendulum of a grandfather clock.

The wings slice upward through the formless gray. A rain shower spatters on the windshield. There is no turbulence. Ahead of us, I know, are mountains, high ones, but in a few minutes we will be above their summits. Guadalajara is forty-five minutes away and possibly it will be clear. Possibly not. Mexican telephones and reporting systems being what they are, I could have learned as easily about the weather on the far side of Saturn as Guadalajara. I do not really care. I have plenty of fuel, know this run as well as a housewife knows the walk from sink to refrigerator. Guadalajara has instrument approaches, but if the weather is below minimums even for those I have a dozen alternate strategies. Only engine failure is a matter for real concern, and I have more faith in this great-hearted lion of a Pratt than I do myself.

Often people ask me if I am not afraid of flying a single-engine craft, and more than once I have had passengers change their minds about a trip when they discovered the ship had only one motor. Laymen and many pilots assume that engines are like cash in bank accounts, the more the safer, and while the idea has its undeniable virtues, in my sort of flying there are a number of extenuating circumstances. Not least among them is money. Any twin able to match the Staggerwing in speed and carrying capacity and climb would cost six times as much new, and probably three or four times as much to run, if you consider the added expenses of much shorter periods between overhauls for the engines, the extra engine, and higher octane fuel. And unless the twin were turbocharged, which would up its initial cost by one-fifth, it would be unable to maintain altitude on one engine over fully three quarters of the routes the yellow bird and I fly, would, for example, assume the characteristics of a slightly powered glider at our present altitude with only one prop pulling. Also, there is not a civilian twin made that can operate from several of the short, unimproved, high-altitude strips the Staggerwing handles as easily as an eagle might perch on a mountain crag, and a number of other strips we use regularly and safely would be marginal propositions at best. So, like many men before me, I am well content to pin my fate on the last part of the old psalm, "Trust in God and Pratt and Whitney."

We continue climbing. En route we may break out on top, but I do not count on it. We have hardly had a glimpse of blue in a month; this is the zenith of the rainy season, and my guess is that we will see neither earth nor sky again until a few moments before touch down. I am confident of the outcome of our journey, yet I am not wholly comfortable. The truth is that I do not like instrument flying. High performance airplanes must be useful if they are to be at all. That is a fact of economics. I could never afford the Staggerwing if she were not able to take me where I need to go under almost any meteorological circumstances, quickly and with a minimum of fuss, but I do not care for timed turns, black boxes, bearings, localizers, radials, glideslopes, beacons, binders thick with approach plates, the alphabet soup of VORs, MDAs, ADFs, DHs, ILSs, HATs, all the addenda of blind navigation. It smacks too much of the age of computers. I would rather fly instruments here in Mexico than in the United States simply because there are fewer planes and no control except on airline routes and near major terminals. I am thrown on my own resources here; there will be no succor in emergency, but that possibility is more than balanced by the freedom.

We pass through 11,000 feet. The local mountain tops are a good 1000 feet below us. I adjust the radios to Guadalajara frequencies. As soon as the needles on the navigation set twitch with life I will try to call, obtain destination weather and a clearance. I plan to level off at 12,000, an altitude which I know will put us 1500 feet above any peak within twenty-five miles of our route. Later, if it becomes necessary to detour to Uruapan or Apatzingán, we will have to go much higher.

"How's Susan?" I ask.

"Asleep," Douglas says.

"You want to fly?"

He looks at me archly over the tops of his glasses. "Are you crazy?"

I often let him steer during cruise. As yet he is too short to reach the rudder pedals, and I have never given him any instrument instruction. Still, he reads a great deal about airplanes, can match me fact for esoteric fact in conversation, and it is understood between us that he will become a pilot.

"Well, maybe you're not quite ready for actual IFR."

Back and forth, back and forth move my eyes. Everything is normal. This is really very easy, at least when there is no turbulence or ice, when your engine is healthy, and you carry six hours of fuel in reserve. I make a minor adjustment to the elevator trim and fold my arms across my chest. The bird flies on rock steady even without my touch. Douglas eyes me skeptically.

"See," I say. "Nothing to it. These old ones were so stable they didn't need autopilots."

"Sure. It's calm. I'd like to see you do it if we were in a thunderstorm."

Eleven thousand eight hundred and what have we here? The clouds are definitely thinning, gray of wet concrete changes to a film of milk. Suddenly we pop out. The vista is awful, in the literal sense of the word, like nothing I have ever seen before.

Technically we are between layers, for many thousands of feet above is another deck of clouds. Below is a lumpy plain of the familiar grimy cotton. But between the sky is like some vast cathedral, an enclosed yet nearly infinite space suffused with incredibly subtle lighting. I have long thought that whoever is in charge of heavenly effects is a great if wasteful artist, a genius in the use of primary colors on massive canvases, but rarely is he moved to attempt the delicate. You expect him to overwhelm you with brightness and dazzle, not something like this.

The air is alive with sea colors and pastels in stained-glass tones, aquamarine blues and greens, a masterful tint of crimson in an upper corner; there are dozens, no hundreds, of vaporous rainbows, which arch around us in profusion, form long corridors and vaults of stupendous height. Tendrils of cloud hang suspended, glowing lavender and turquoise and pale green as if lit from within.

I level us off, trim the bird and make power adjustments and lean the

19

mixture, check the operation of the mags and carb heat, but it is all I can do to wrest my attention from the world outside. I bend across to Douglas so that I can speak to him in a whisper.

"Wake Susan."

He nods, twists between the seats like an eel. In a moment he belts back in and I feel my wife's hand on my shoulder. I turn and she smiles.

We fly on through a mounting impression of quiet. The Pratt rumbles, the airflow hisses, yet we seem to move in stately and ethereal silence, a ghost ship running with the wind down some skyscape from a dream. This is a place never intended for human beings. Lindbergh said that flying was sometimes "like a vision at the end of life forming a bridge to death." He must have had some morning like this one in mind. Perhaps this is a glimpse of eternity. I am in no way a churchgoer, in fact except for weddings and funerals have not set foot in one since prep school and loathsome mornings of compulsory chapel, but I think this is the kind of feeling the great Catholic architects must have been trying to inspire. If the builders of Chartres could see this they would understand and feel very inadequate.

Beneath us now are a few breaks. Through one we see a little Mexican hill town, tile roofs and cobblestones and whitewash and the inevitable church. Somehow it is in direct sunlight. Pink stone is transformed to living blood. A little later we see a breast-shaped mountain, also in sunlight. It is a green twice as bright as an ad for bluegrass seed, deep as an Iowa sky at midsummer dusk. A field of the Lord if man ever saw one. The gaps close, the big yellow bird glides on.

Thirty minutes pass and we are still open-mouthed with awe, not yet accustomed to the sublime variety of this new realm. We point fingers at each tangle of rainbows and hall of violet cloud stalactites as if to reassure ourselves they are not mirages; occasionally our path leads through a feathery scrap of cloud and the cabin is filled with a dozen misty colors. A rainbow curves away from our lower wing, near enough so that I could roll down the window and grab a handful.

But the radio picks up the Guadalajara omni station strongly, and it is time to think about coming down. Earphones on, a crackle of static. Communications set to approach control. I give our identification, position, altitude, ask for weather. I speak in English, the international language of aeronautics — theoretically the control tower personnel in Timbuktu should be able to speak English.

"Beech five four three," the controller says. "Weather Guadalajara is seven hundred foots overcast. Raining light. One mile visibility. You make the instrument approach?"

"Yes."

"Hokay. You clear for instrument approach runway two eight. Call the tower outbound. Altimeter two nine nine eight. No other traffic."

I repeat, motion Douglas to get my book of approach charts. A last long look around and we sink back into the clouds. Our personal rainbow dissolves away from the wing root. The altimeter unwinds, a scientific recording of descent from the supernatural. My eyes take up their sliding rhythm across the panel, pause to make sure the book is opened to the right page. We are enveloped in gray again and noises assume their normal proportions. Susan is right. It is cozy in here, familiar and comforting after what we have seen. Five minutes pass. A flag on an instrument flips, now says FROM instead of TO. We have crossed the station; through the clouds below is the airport. I dial the tower, say, "Five four three outbound for procedure turn."

"Five four three report procedure turn inbound."

"Procedure turn inbound."

I twist a knob, turn the plane to a new heading, reduce power. Carb heat on. Punch the stopwatch button on the dashboard clock. We are descending steadily to 8500. Monitor head temperatures so they do not cool too quickly. Richen mixture gradually. Three minutes on the stopwatch. I take up a new heading. Another minute, another turn.

I discover that I am enjoying this as I never have instrument work. The little series of mathematical problems succumbs to precise mechanical maneuvers. Everything the bird and I do is quantifiable, explicable, a clear result of specific action. This time the process makes me aware of myself, who I am and what I am capable of, in a way that is very pleasant.

"Five four three procedure turn inbound two eight."

"Report runway in sight."

The Staggerwing locks on the inbound heading, slides down the undimensioned gray. Six thousand feet. We should break out soon. I glance up, still the gray cloak. I review the missed approach procedure mentally. Five thousand eight hundred.

"Runway in sight," Douglas says.

"Good boy."

Rain patters at glass. Ahead is a long slab of black asphalt. It glistens luminously in the wet. I lower the gear, twist with my crank to make sure it is down and locked. In moisture it is wise to place no faith in the yellow bird's electrical system. I have seen it short out in heavy dew. Flaps down.

22

"Five four three has the runway."

"Clear to land."

We cross the threshold. Nose up. A tad of throttle. The Staggerwing floats on, spinner rising and the rate of sink decreasing with every millimeter we drop. This runway is forever, the longest in Mexico, no need to plunk down in the first hundred feet. I make the best landing of my life. The three wheels touch, but we cannot feel the contact. The airspeed bleeds off to zero. Otherwise the only clue that we are not still flying is a watery hiss, the tires aquaplaning.

We taxi to parking. The prop twirls through inertia revolutions into silence. Rain taps on the fabric. The gyros whine. We sit for fully two minutes, unable or not wanting to talk. Finally Susan leans forward, kisses me on the cheek. I reach over, ruffle Douglas's hair, a gesture he finds especially annoying. He punches me on the arm.

"Mongers, man," he says. "That was better than 'Star Trek.'"

The three of us laugh aloud.

3

Those that I fight I do not hate,
Those that I guard I do not love;
. . . .
No likely end could bring them loss
Or leave them happier than before.
Nor law, nor duty bade me fight,
Nor public men, nor cheering crowds,
A lonely impulse of delight
Drove to this tumult in the clouds;
. . . .

— William Butler Yeats
An Irish Airman Foresees His Death

So flying is fun and sometimes it is magic, but of course it is not always a joyous romp or an excursion to a hallowed place. Every pilot with a slight accumulation of hours in his log has had his trying times in the air, occasions when he matched nerve and wits against the weather, or cursed and sweated and perhaps prayed a bit, if that was in his nature, as mechanical matters went sour, or the times when his judgment was less than perfect and he reviewed a flight with new knowledge of the limits of mortality and the byways of luck. But the passage of even a little time is apt to alter perspective, and what was frightening becomes enlightening in memory, what was desperate achieves the status of interesting.

It seemed to me for a long time that all aeronautical endeavors, not simply the pleasurable or the beautiful ones, were protected by a unique quality, an aura of sanctuary and haven, that made them immune from the manifold taints of earthly enterprise. I suppose you could say I refused to evaluate the obvious, but Hiroshima was for documentaries about Harry Truman, and jet noise afflicted people who made stupid real estate investments. The sky, as far as I was concerned, was completely the refuge of grace and innocence. I was in love with flying — no other phrase is appropriate —for many years before I became a pilot, the more so afterward, infatuated, bewitched, blind as any smitten swain to the grossest blemishes and failings, until an odd set of circumstances conspired to tarnish the miracle. The series of events, if not traumatic, was certainly etched into my awareness and could not help but alter it.

26   The place is Phuc Vinh, a district capital in the province of Tay Ninh, and base for the 1/9 Cavalry, a legendary helicopter outfit. The hub of life here is the airfield with its lines of revetments occupied by the various breeds of chopper: sedate sedan-like Hueys; little dragonfly Hughes Loaches, scout ships, the sporty cars of the rotary-wing world; sway-backed twin rotor Chinooks; and predatory Cobra gunships.

I am walking down a flight line from an operations shack with two pilots and gunner. We are about to commence a mission whose prospect at this moment pleases no one. It has been laid on for my benefit — I am a reporter and a colonel translated my casual request to fly in a Cobra into an opportunity to demonstrate the facility with which he could make things happen. The pilots are resentful, mainly toward the colonel, and I am embarrassed that I should cause them discomfort.

It is early afternoon and very hot, an acetylene heat of cloying equatorial dampness, enervating and grating, abrasive as a jungle sore. The air has an oily touch. Tarmac and treelines writhe and shimmer at the tip of the sun's torch. Our clothes, olive-drab flight suits of a scratchy fire-resistant fabric permeated with asbestos, chafe wetly at crotches and armpits. We have eaten less than an hour ago and the gaseous residue of beans and soggy franks grinds in my stomach.

"Shit," shouts one of the pilots. "Every gook with any intelligence whatsoever will be asleep in some nice cool bunker."

"I'm really sorry about this," I reply, also in a shout.

"Shit."

We walk on, carrying our heavy armored breastplates and helmets and maps. The pilots are further burdened with pistols and gunbelts.

We shout because it is impossible to make yourself understood at any lower volume. Your hearing, from first light to last, if you stay near the flight line, is assaulted by the chopper sounds, a never ending mechanical madness. The Turbine Overture of 1969. Turbines whir winding up, the whir evolves into a scream; the odor of burned kerosene pervades the air; rotors begin a ponderous stately gyration, accelerate into blur and slap at you with the chopachopachopa of a bird pulling pitch and lifting off, a sound at once sharp and flat that reminds me of being a boy and attaching pieces of cardboard to the fork of my bicycle in such a manner that they would smack each passing spoke. The choppers are much louder, make the sound with the authority of incalculable power. Other turbines lull you into momentary relief with a dying dynamo whine as they spool down.

Sometimes the chopper turbines are underscored by the arrival or departure of a C–130, a lurching guppy-bulbous turboprop transport that shrieks in singularly demented fashion, sounds while merely taxiing like the agony of some monstrous animal in extremis, the death cry sustained of a disembowled rhino. Rarely the turbines are counterpointed by the nostalgic melodies of piston engines, the out-of-place civilian buzz of O–1 spotters, little two-place, high-wing Cessnas looking like extras from a very low-budget war movie, and the soothing other-era rumble of a DeHaviland Caribou's radials.

Two or three times a day you are subjected to a crescendo. A platoon, or perhaps even a company of infantry, will appear in battle dress, men trussed and sagging under the weight of steel pots and full canteens, pockets swollen with ammo clips, bandoliers of 7.62 worn like necklaces and black weapons, throats scarved against sweat and insects with OD towels. They form in a loose circle to be briefed by an officer, then break into groups of eight. A brace of Hueys lights up, beats the dust to a wicked filthy froth, a miasma, a tempest of cosmic proportion. The infantry groups hump their shoulders and drop their heads and drive forward into the maws of rotor blast. In unison the ships lift off, a chop flap formation thunderscream, a terrible multiplication and compounding of noises, tortured air roiling around tortured machinery, overwhelming impossible clumps of sound that strike you with tangible force, like concussion, that beat and stomp and buffet and shrivel you and dissipate after a second, fade to a syncopated pop-pop as the machines arrow out over the perimeter.

Then perhaps a moment of pure silence, an instant of respite between movements, cool and sweet to the canals of the inner ear as spring water to a parched throat. But down the line of plate steel and sandbag revetments, all filmed by settling dust and undulating like mirage in the sun and residue of exhaust, the blades of a Cobra cleave the air like precisely wielded machetes.

We arrive at our ships, conduct the preflight inspection. I am flying front seat in a Cobra, watch carefully as the pilot does his walk around. The plane has a rakish beak which culminates in a chin turret housing a minigun, the snout of a bird of prey with unusual extra talons mounted in its craw. Rockets holstered in round pods ride the ship's waist. The canopies are tinted blue like fishbowls in a discothèque. The crew chief watches the pilot, as crew chiefs always have, with a mixture of apprehension that he may have overlooked something obvious or vital and a dash of condescension. Mechanics know their machines far better than pilots, yet the pilots luxuriate in rank and glory.

We climb the steep sides to the cockpits. The chief pushes vigorously on my leg, a well-intentioned boost that nearly sends me sprawling head first into the seat. For a moment I am furious, but quickly the heat smothers my emotion. I squirm in, thread my legs over the collective and cyclic sticks and around the octopus-armed reflector gunsight. The chief helps me arrange shoulder straps and seat belt, places the breastplate, which rests on my lap, uncomfortably heavy. I assure him I am capable of closing the canopy by myself. I put the helmet on. It is a hateful confining weight in this heat, and because it is a quarter size too small it immediately begins to crimp my ears painfully. I plug in the microphone and headset jack, but the radio is dead still.

I sit there encased, armored, immobilized, and incommunicado, simmering in the drip of my own juices, helpless as a mailed knight shackled

29

to a dead horse, and curse the stupidity of my predicament. This flight will be pointless, prove nothing. The pilot was right about everyone intelligent being asleep in a bunker — the Vietnamese on both sides tend to relax during the heat of the day.

Yet I am counting on that habit, or I would never have accepted the colonel's arrangement. I am a noncombatant, a civilian, emphatically so, but in a Cobra I shall have to shoot if we find something. In other ships a correspondent may travel as observer; in this one you are part of the crew, for there are only two seats, and each occupant is responsible for the operation of one weapons system. I have flown in Cobras before, but always on practice hops. The prospective problem does not weigh heavily on me now, the odds against action are too long; I simply feel tired and uncomfortable, annoyed that I am here, carried along by events I am too lethargic to struggle against.

But such thought trains hint at a curious, and, to me, significant fact — we correspondents hold the strangest of ethical terrains in this war. I, and most of my press friends, disapprove of the war as much as any bearded beaded protester, and with better reason, for we know a number of its hideous facets intimately. Napalm, that catchword of the activists, and white phosphorous and refugees and rocket attacks, the corrupt incompetence of our allies, the racial frictions and stupefying boredoms, the official lying and the sweat in your eyes pack on your back left foot right foot leech on the leg life of the grunts, the whole endless catalogue of miseries and frustrations, are not just abstract curdles of the conscience teleprompted by the evening news. It is true that we are party to the excitement of war, attracted, some of us, by its darkest fascinations, drawn to its undeniable quickenings and heightenings, victim as often as soldiers to its violent whims, but we are in no way responsible for them, so that through all I have witnessed during two tours here I have been able to keep a strong partition erected between events and the most cherished corner of myself.

Perhaps that partition might seem a self-righteous moral superiority, a trace of the prig, but to me it is very important, the keystone in my concept of self. I want very much to be a knowledgeable man, able to write about Vietnam — clearly the central issue of the times, the problem and the event to which all others are satellites — from a citadel made unassailable by the breadth and depth of my experience. I have many friends in the military about whose esteem I care, and it suits me well if they see me as eccentric, but not cowardly. Yet, like most other younger reporters, I want a clear disassociation from the policies of my government. Hence we usually refer to the Americans in the same tone as the North Vietnamese, as if by inflection we can make foreigners of our own people, strangers to be observed and discussed with cool objectivity.

Active abetment of their operations is virtually unthinkable. The best reporters will go anywhere, no matter the danger, or perhaps because of it — I sometimes think my friends, especially the photographers, are a little like the bravest protesters of 1968, doubly determined to prove their physical courage because they do not wear a uniform — but not for my generation the Hemingway fantasy realized of leading troops, some Indochinese version of the dash on Paris at the head of Maquis irregulars. Detachment is too nearly synonymous with self-respect.

But of course wars are the least controllable of human activities, and the most deeply respected intentions often become the casualties of events. A friend of mine, a photographer who was captured in Cambodia, told me a story which illustrates the occasional difficulty of our position. He once spent several months with a Special Forces A team in a remote corner of the country. The unit was composed of the usual twelve Americans and a hundred or so Nungs and Cambodes. My friend patrolled with them, ate and slept and went drinking with them, was mortared with them and helped tend their wounded, tweezed ticks from their flesh and whored beside them, became in almost every way a fully accepted member of their family, until one fight in which they captured a dozen Viet Cong. The government troops set about torturing their prisoners to death, an activity to which the Americans lent tacit approval. My friend took pictures of the torturers and the dying and the Americans, who stood grouped a little way off with their backs turned, like schoolmasters at a nasty but necessary lower-class initiation, photographed frantically, burned roll after roll of film, as if the camera lens could shield him from his own vision, watched the slow knife work through the instrument of his objectivity until he could bear to watch no longer, and then he borrowed a pistol from one of the Americans and executed the last seven prisoners. Several thanked him for his mercy before he shot them.

"You all set?" My earphones are alive, the voice of the man in the back seat comes through them against a sidetone of light static and hum.

I key the mike button on the cyclic. "Rog."

"O.K. Shut the canopy."

We lock in, the blades begin to sweep in front of us, the instruments jump and jiggle into life. The machine shudders. The pilot eases out of the revetment, and I follow with my hands and feet held lightly on the controls. This is a difficult task, for the walls of the revetment are no more than three feet from our skids and the slightest miscalculation will hook us. I have seen two helicopters flagellate themselves to deformed twists of metal attempting to perform the operation. At speed there is nothing tricky about flying choppers; they behave like mildly sensitive airplanes, but hovering requires a dexterity I cannot help but admire.

A few hundred feet down the line a Loach has backed out of its revetment and now runs a hover check. It is Cavalier One Zero, and will be our scout ship on this mission. My pilot is Cavalier Two Two, and our Cobra is the flying artillery.

"Your reflector working?" he asks.

I peer into the sight. In its bowels are little points of light, barely discernible. "Affirm."

"One Zero, Two Two," he says to the Loach. "You ready?"

"Cavalier One Zero. That's a Rog."

We call tower, get wind and altimeter setting, density altitude, a clearance to take off.

"Cavalier Two Two. What's the redleg doing?"

"Negative artillery reported at this time, sir," the tower says.

Helicopter pilots, all pilots, in Vietnam must consider the possibility of flying through an artillery shoot when they operate at low levels. An acquaintance of mine witnessed the destruction of a Caribou which passed near the trajectory of a shell with a proximity fuse. He told me the biggest piece left was a lump of aluminum about the size of a clenched fist.

We head out. Two Two holds us low for a few moments while the Cobra accelerates, then lifts away from the deck in a hard graceful climb. Cobras are the quietest of helicopters — most military choppers do not have doors and you are continually subjected to the waterfall roar of slipstream and rotorwash — and the smoothest, the vibrator effect soothed to a faint flap flap as the blades change pitch. The air becomes cooler with a little altitude, and I breathe deeply. My clothes are soaked through, however, and I can feel streams of sweat squirming down my sides.

We pass the perimeter of the base, called the green line, tangles of barb wire and fighting holes and tank positions and trenches and a broad

33

stripe carefully kept clear of all vegetation, an effort to rob the enemy of concealment. Our government and the South Vietnamese have declared this whole area safe and secure at least a half dozen times within my memory, but no one who must live or work in it would agree. Several weeks in the future a close friend of mine, a man who has spent nearly four years in this country, will have his skull punctured by shrapnel from a booby trap near here.

The Loach stays on the deck. It will be his job to follow trails, to sniff at bunker openings, correlate and evaluate a thousand little details. Good Loach pilots have the same sensitivity to signs of physical presence as a frontier scout and are highly prized. Their work is also very dangerous. They fly low and slow and their machines are small and lightly armed and armored. For some reason Loach pilots always seem to be very young, fuzzy-lipped nineteen-year-olds, warrant officers, clear-eyed high school quarterbacks who were not quite talented enough to attract a college scholarship and went into the Army instead.

The boy commanding Cavalier One Zero this afternoon is no exception. He is quiet and shy and is called Wimpy by the others. The sweetness of his face is marred only by traces of acne beneath his cheek bones and blackheads on the tip of his nose.

"You want to fly?" Two Two asks me.

"Sure."

"You've got it. Just follow the Loach."

"Roger that."

34   We cruise over a bruised landscape, paddy land dented by countless shell and bomb craters inflicted in what appears to be a completely random pattern. We chat in the abbreviated phrases of working pilots. After the first few minutes of unfamiliarity with the feel of the controls I slip into

a well-known and comfortable state, alert to the instruments and the Loach below us, but with a corner of my mind left free to think, to fantasize, to contemplate. I might as well be at home in my own ship.

My physical discomfiture is forgotten. I am flying, therefore I am content. It is possible to ignore the true implications of the terrain beneath, of the machine gun between my feet, the rockets at my hips. The helmet no longer cruelly twists my ears; the boom mike in front of my mouth lends a nice professional touch. I daydream, imagine myself a fighter pilot on patrol. The land below is Surrey or Kent in the Valhalla summer of 1940. I scan the sky for ME–109s, and my thumb rests on the gun button of a Spitfire, that noble symbol from the last righteous war.

A slight movement of the cyclic, an infinitesimal back pressure on the collective, and the Cobra soars elegantly. I tip the nose, the airspeed needle plummets around the dial. I am tempted to dive for the Loach's tail and fasten there, dare him to escape by what means he can. Perhaps Two Two knows what I am thinking.

"She flies O.K., doesn't she?" he says.

"Affirm."

I wheel the ship from a steep bank left to a steep bank right. She is responsive to a degree, powerful and harmonious, a thoroughbred of a warbird. When I was a kid my leading fantasy was to be a military pilot. It usually far eclipsed even major baseball stardom. I made models of World War II fighter planes, hung them by nearly invisible threads from the vigas in my room. I used to lie for hours on my bed and watch them turn, a lazily rotating galaxy of lean square-tipped P–51s, crank-winged Corsairs, perfectly proportioned Zeros and FW–190s. They were triggers to a thousand daydreams, instant transport to a cold perfect blue world of freedom and delight.

My mother's only brother, after whom I am named, was a Navy pilot in the infancy of carrier aviation and later a stress engineer and test pilot. My mother's room was my favorite in our house because its walls were hung with photos of old Boeing and Chance Vought biplanes, dive bombers with Felix the Cat crouching puckishly on the fuselage, a cartoon bomb with lit fuse held in one paw, and rows of grave young men with wings of Navy gold on their breasts grouped in front of propellers stopped perfectly horizontal. The airplanes adumbrated dope and the aroma of hot oil and the banshee howl of wind in wires down across the years — I could all but feel the clatter and throb of those uncowled radials — and the young men were the finest distillate of camaraderie, adventure shared, costume brawls crossing the equator and phosphorescent wakes beneath the Southern Cross, launches from pitching decks and crash barriers and formation rolls; and in the photos also were echoes of the ships, names redolent with gallant traditions, the *Lexington* and especially the *Sara,* and the squadrons, Bombing Two, Fighting Six, history I could see, heritage I could not help but absorb. When we visited my uncle's grave to place Christmas wreaths my mother always cried and I tried to comfort her manfully while hoping in secret that my tombstone would have wings and a propeller carved in the granite too.

My favorite radio program was "Twelve O'Clock High." It came on past my bedtime and I used to evade maternal wrath by covering both my head and the instrument with pillows to deaden the sounds of aerial combat. Later, in my early teens, I joined the Ground Observer Corps, a 1950s spawn of the Cold War, and spent countless afternoons in the glass-walled tower of the state capitol building a block from my parents' house in Santa Fe. We mainly reported sedate Pioneer and Continental DC–3s inbound for the Santa Fe airport from Denver, but one afternoon the tower was buzzed by a pair of F–86 interceptors from Albuquerque. The Observer squadron leader, an adult who prided himself on his skill with recognition photos, happened to be present, and he manned the hot line, informed the authorities that Santa Fe was under siege by a wing of Lockheed Shooting Stars. I grabbed the phone from his hand, and shouted, "They're North American Sabres. F–86 Dogs. They're *not* Shooting Stars." My voice broke into a horrible adolescent squeak halfway through.

One time my younger brother was in the hospital for an operation, and a family friend, a crusty professional pilot who had flown with the Royal Air Force in World War II, gave him a pair of British wings and a much tarnished medal. My brother, who then as now manifests aversion for flight in any form, turns green when I offer to take him up for a session of aerobatics, pinned them both on his pajama shirt, and I was furious with jealousy. I smile remembering and honk the Cobra through a hard S turn.

"Two Two. One Zero." Wimpy's voice breaks my reverie, has taken on a high unnatural pitch. "I got gooks down here."

"There shouldn't be any friendlies here."

"Roger that. They look like friendlies."

"I got it," Two Two says to me. "Figure the grid coordinates."

"O.K.," I say. "You better check them too."

"They're shooting at me," Wimpy says.

"Where are they?"

"The fuckers are firing."

The Loach is jinking around a ragged right-hand circle below us.

"My three o'clock now."

"What are the coordinates?"

I struggle with my map, recalcitrant and unpliable in a plastic casing, try to find a reference from which I can figure accurately.

"I'm working on them."

My mind spins quickly, the center antenna focused on the problem of defining our position for the artillery; the radio babble nags at the edge of awareness, a rasp that demands occasional attention; and an eye within my mind's eye views the whole proceeding with near frantic alarm. I feel as though I am trying unsuccessfully to juggle three objects of entirely different dimension. A pulse flicks wildly in my temple.

"One Zero, you still taking fire?"

"Negative. My gunner's douching them."

I try to shut out everything but the map, a scramble of multishaded green and lines and symbols with precise grid squares superimposed, all of it gone unaccountably incomprehensible to me. You read military maps right and up. Or is it left and down.

"Cease fire. Cease fire." An unfamiliar voice stabs through our headsets.

"Who's that?"

"Somebody on the emergency freq."

"Cease fire. This is Spearhead Six. Tell that Loach to quit shooting."

Wimpy has flushed and shot at a South Vietnamese unit. Spearhead Six is the senior American advisor.

"You're not supposed to be here," Two Two says.

"Bullshit."

Recriminations fill the airways for five minutes before we beat a retreat. Spearhead Six is undoubtedly at least a captain, while Wimpy and Two Two are merely warrant officers, so they are not about to press the issue of who is supposed to be where. Fortunately Wimpy's gunner has inflicted no casualties. As we head off, Wimpy says in the privacy of our frequency, "The fuckers were shooting at us and they wasn't even supposed to be there."

"You're sure they were firing?" I ask.

"Fucking A I'm sure. Fucking useless dinks."

"They do it all the time," Two Two says.

"Dear Mom," Wimpy says, "Got my balls blown off by a gook on our side. He thought I was an NVA bird."

"No he didn't," Two Two says. "He was just bored. Dinks get bored easy and then they shoot at us."

I do not join the banter, sit quiet in my front cockpit and feel relief wash over me. Also shame that I was so incompetent with the map. I have as much experience in map reading as Two Two and Wimpy combined, yet the simplest principles were beyond my grasp when it mattered. I offer myself the small consolation that I was not so afraid of being shot at as shooting, and salve the wounds to my airman's vanity by imagining how I shall relate the experience to my colleagues of the press in Saigon. "How were things with the Cav?" "Fucked up as usual. I went out in a Cobra and we got in a fight with an ARVN unit."

Then I feel small and petty and frivolous, a dilettante tampering in matters of blood and bone.

We fly on. Two Two and One Zero outdo each other coining epithets for our Vietnamese allies, for advisors, for infantry, for all who do not fly. I cannot tell if they are very tough and blasé, or frightened at the near catastrophe and working to cover it. Perhaps both.

For myself, I just want this to be over, to return to Phuc Vinh. Two Two gives me the ship again, though I think I detect condescension in his voice, a mild reprimand for my lack of dexterity with the map. I fly, but without the usual sense of control and oneness with the machine.

39

I feel as awkward as a student on first solo, guided only by a few hours' experience and stray threads of theoretical knowledge.

The country is open and flat now, not heavily vegetated. It is pocked with American firebases, encampments of earthworks and sandbags and concertina housing artillery, gashes of ocher in the dusty green. Broad dirt roads connect the bases. The trees covering the spaces between are narrow and stunted, look stickery. We follow trails that meander like animal paths. Perhaps they are, but probably not. This is one of the major infiltration routes from Cambodia. Rumors have it that the North Vietnamese drive Soviet trucks along some of these roads at night.

The Loach darts like a hummingbird, stops and hovers over a suspicious spot, accelerates off on a tangent, skids along the brow of a low hill, climbs up for a general look at the terrain and dips back down to a trail. I fly lazy covering patterns. I am getting myself back in hand, assure myself that nothing more will happen. When our fuel reaches a certain state the Loach will climb and we'll go home. The pulse in my temple is subsiding.

Then, incubus reanimated, comes Wimpy's voice with the unmistakable urgency, "I've got gooks."

"You sure, One Zero?" Two Two asks.

"Fuck you. Look down here. They're on the trail. Maybe a fucking company."

In the background of One Zero's transmissions we can hear his crewman's machine gun clattering.

We circle twice. Two Two takes back control. "You're armed," he tells me, meaning he has activated the circuits which fire the minigun. He has been following the map closely, calls a nearby firebase with coordinates, tells the artillery to stand by. "Get your ass out of there," he says to the Loach.

"Rog. Douche the trail. They're all along it."

We wing over for a run. The Cobra drops down the sky like a plummet. Two Two begins firing rockets. They leave the pods with a crackle whoosh, like striking a kitchen match near your ear and speed ahead of us trailing erratic wisps of smoke. The earth is swelling in my windscreen, but I am not alarmed. It is no different than diving at a cow in some isolated field, a pastime I have pursued often. The first rockets strike the trail in quick flashes, small, decorative-looking. I can see people running, but no details of their dress or expression. We are moving too fast. I am listening for the twangs of ground fire, hear none. Two Two pulls us up in a zoom to the left, I feel a little G, but it is nothing compared to a run in a fighter bomber or even strenuous aerobatics in a civilian plane.

"Take a look-see," Two Two says.

"Rog," Wimpy says.

"How many do you think?" Two Two asks me.

"I don't know." I had seen no more than four or five.

"A fucking company at least. Douche down that trail when I tell you."

"You got two or three," the Loach reports.

"Get out of there," Two Two says. "I want to let the reporter work out."

The Cobra navigates another circle above the area. "Now," Two Two says. A moment's hesitation and a deep breath are my only concessions to the difficulties of the moment. There is no time for consideration. It is strange, especially in view of my recent panic and funk, but I am almost calm. I am aware that what I am about to do is something I shall not be able to undo, that this moment represents a demarcation line of significance, that to cross it will make a difference, perhaps make me different, but it is as if these thoughts are in the mind of someone else, sensed by me but reasoned elsewhere, and the possibility of choice is no

41

possibility at all. I center the trail in the pips of light, squeeze the trigger. A wild whirring from the nose, a sound not unlike an electric appliance. Waterfalls of tracer like a Fourth of July extravaganza in some small Midwestern town spill toward the ground in an unhurried arc, arrive, ricochet. I move the dots up the trail slowly. It is like watering an ant path with a garden hose gushing sparklers.

"All right," Two Two says. "That ain't half-bad shooting for a civilian."

We climb a little, call in the artillery. First come the pale mushrooms of white phosphorous rounds, markers, followed by the huge flame-cored detonations of the high explosive, 105 and 155 mm. The explosions reach us even a half mile away, concussions slap the ship, cause a tingling in the sinuses. Some of the rounds are delay, penetrate deep and then erupt in enormous geysers of dirt. The idea is to destroy bunkers.

The radios are busy to the saturation point. It is worse than an approach to O'Hare on a murky busy night. Everyone wants in on our act. An Air Force Forward Air Controller, one of the little Cessnas, is hurrying toward us, the prelude to a fighter-bomber strike. The artillery is coming from two different firebases, and Two Two is adjusting the aims of both batteries. Base, Phuc Vinh control, is listening. I recognize the voice of the colonel offering irrelevant advice, unnecessary exhortation.

Twice again I am called on to fire the minigun. I squeeze the trigger and the high-speed dishwasher imparts a gentle vibration to my hand and arm. The nose spews bright pinheads. During one firing I think, quite dispassionately, that now the North Vietnamese will have every right to shoot me if we are forced down. We are too high for me to know what I am hitting, but Wimpy says, "Four for the reporter. We ought to draft him."

Another section of Cobras arrives, code named the Blue Maxes. They are artillery ships, carry extra rockets in place of a portion of fuel. Two Two reports to base, "At this time we have a checkfire on the redleg and Blue Max is doing his thing." We circle, the Loach circles, the Blue Max Cobras circle and roll into rocket runs, and the Air Force FAC circles. I have never seen so many aircraft wandering in such proximity. We are supposed to be layered, but nobody seems to be paying any attention at all to separation. Two Two turns to the right in order to watch a Blue Max in a run. Out of the corner of my left eye I catch movement. A frozen moment of sheerest terror, ultimate extract of paralyzing horror. My throat makes a sound like gargling. It is another Blue Max following his friend in a run. We are about to fly right in front of him. I grab the controls and yank. After an eon of delay our ship skids frantically. The second Blue Max is shooting, rockets flick past us, the propellant debris spatters against our nose skin. It sounds like a handful of sand thrown on tin. Then the Cobra hurtles by, close enough for us to make out the stenciled instructions on its fuel cover caps. Both of the pilots are looking straight ahead, absorbed in what they are doing. "Jesus," Two Two says.

The Blue Maxes fly off, ammunition expended. Wimpy darts back onto the trail, now shrouded in a pall of dust and smoke.

"How many more?" Two Two asks.

No answer.

"Is he all right?" I ask.

"Sure," Two Two says. "He's probably killing somebody. He never talks when he's killing somebody."

After a time Wimpy announces there are nine bodies on the trail. No movement visible. Two Two calls in more artillery. The batteries report they're low on ammunition. "Bullfuck," Wimpy says. Two Two tells the firebases he's crediting them with two kills apiece, that he's sorry they

43

can't keep up the good work. "Those are your kills," he says to me. "Sometimes those dickheads get hurty feelings if you don't play a little kissass." Soon new and intense barrages roll into the area.

We are low on fuel, race away to a nearby auxiliary strip and top our tanks. Back on station in fifteen minutes. The artillery continues. Finally the Air Force jets arrive. We move well to the side, put another checkfire on the guns. The FAC marks targets with colored rockets. The jets, Cessna A–37s from Bien Hoa, roll into their bomb runs, steep plunging dives that look almost vertical followed by pullouts of lofty grace. They almost Immelmann going out. After his last pass the jet leader does a lazy barrel roll. The FAC and the jets are in a politeness contest.

"Hawkeye Nine," says the jet leader. "It's been a real pleasure working with you."

"Likewise. You did some real fine bombing."

"Thank you much. Stop by and see us."

"I'll do that. You do same if you get to Papa Victor."

The jets, low on fuel after less than an hour aloft, arrow off, in an instant reduce themselves to the dimension of bug specks on our windscreens. The Loach goes back in yet again, reports five new bodies, and "a fucking black pajama top on top of one of these trees."

"Any sign of the bod?"

"That's a negative. But we'll give the Air Force another one. Nobody could have lived through that."

I say, "What if it was only laundry?" but no one deigns to answer.

"Hawk Niner," says Wimpy to the FAC. "Now I'm gonna show you some real bombing."

The Loach drops fragmentation grenades on some rice sacks. The explosions are like the flicker of fireflies in the churning gloom.

44

"How you like that?" Wimpy asks.

The FAC, laughing: "You guys scare me. You fly too low."

"You guys scare me. You fly too high."

A last artillery barrage and we start home. Two Two informs base that our final score is seventeen. The colonel announces he is putting Wimpy and Two Two in for medals.

It is almost dark when we get to Phuc Vinh. The runway and taxiways are outlined by smudge pots. Two Two eases into the revetment, the Cobra settles delicately onto the ground, and we sit still, isolated and silent, watching the decelerating blades sweep past against the twilit sky, listening to the long and lonesome whine of the turbine winding down. Then the canopies are opened by hands not our own and we climb stiffly down the sides and the ground crews and other pilots are all around us, slapping our backs, punching our arms, laughing. We have been gone five hours.

We spent an uneasy twenty minutes with the colonel, like star athletes summoned to the principal's office for commendation after a noteworthy triumph. He insisted we take a can of beer with him. Wimpy had reported our final kill total at seventeen, but I noticed the colonel had already exaggerated it to twenty-seven. By the time the briefers in Saigon got hold of the story the count would soar even higher. Afterward, when we had been allowed to leave, Wimpy described the colonel as the "chief flaming anus in the Nam."

Dinner hour was past, but the mess hall was reopened especially for us and we were given steaks and french fries, strawberry ice cream for dessert, a feast for heroes American style. I was very hungry, which surprised me. Other pilots sat with us and there was much mock-envious joking and Two Two and Wimpy went out of their way to praise me. "The dumbass can't read a map for shit but he shoots all right." There was a long and elaborate exposition of a fantasy common to all of them — the North Vietnamese took the field in helicopters and great aerial battles ensued in which each pilot became an ace — and I remember clearly sitting back and looking at them, ten or twelve young pilots, the oldest a captain of perhaps twenty-five (I would mark my own twenty-seventh birthday in two days), and thinking that if you changed the uniforms, fitted them with Sam Brownes and choke collars and tunics of khaki and jodhpur breeches, if you cleared away the Hamms and Nehi cans and substituted bottles of Beaujolais and put a wind-up gramophone on the table, this could be a retake of one of those old photos captioned An RFC Mess Somewhere in France; they could be a Pup squadron during Bloody April, Wimpy an incipient Albert Ball, V.C., the violin-playing Niueport driver who on occasion tried to ram his opponents but was known to his comrades for grave gentleness.

They were obviously willing to accept me, to consider me an initiate of the fellowship, a compliment I found warming in spite of myself. I knew well enough that there would come an introspection of the greatest discomfort, and this was welcome postponement.

Our dinner finished, they drifted off until only Wimpy and I were left. We talked on over tepid orange sodas. Wimpy did not like beer, said, "Anyway, I have to fly tomorrow."

We talked planes for the most part, mentioned the afternoon only briefly. He had learned to fly on fixed-wing craft, had a civilian license, had joined the Army in order to obtain instrument rating, et cetera, the experience and the badges necessary for a career as a professional pilot. He talked of the pleasure of flying in the early morning, taking a Cub or a Luscomb off from a grass field in the Midwest, the runways bright with dew and wisps of condensation forming at the prop tips, floating over the rural countryside on flawless air.

I spoke of mornings in Mexico when I would make an instrument takeoff through ground fog with only needle, ball and airspeed for reference, break out five or seven hundred feet above ground. I would steer toward the sun sometimes, which seemed to hang in the clouds like a fuzzy light bulb the size of a basketball. On top the fog was not smooth, but fluffed, like tightly packed wads of purest cotton, and I would fly along with the belly of the plane submerged, marveling at the sensation of speed and taking delight when the prop would snatch into a snowy outcropping.

We both liked to fly low, chase across fields and hills at speed, tilting between trees. He said that was the part of flying scout ships he liked best, never tired of. We agreed to visit each other when we got home and do some flying together.

Finally he stood up and stretched, said he was going to bed. He walked across the mess hall under the hard yellow glaze of overhead lights, but before he was halfway to the door he turned and came back. He had a cowlick which stood up like a detail from a Norman Rockwell cover, but the lighting cast deep shadows under his eyes, a detail by Goya.

"There's just one thing," he said.

"What's that?"

"When you write this, don't say that I like killing people. You understand? That wouldn't be right."

I laughed, but he said, "No, I mean it."

And walked out.

I sat by myself for a long time, perhaps several hours. I scribbled in my notebook, jotted down the details of the day, though I doubted I should forget a one of them if I lived to be ninety. I also scribbled a number of quasi-philosophical speculations about Wimpy, which was really avoidance of an examination of myself.

War pilots are perhaps the ultimate modernists, I wrote, the perfect existentialists, involved in the moment, devoted to sensation, the esthetics of controlling craft of the highest performance to the complete exclusion of other considerations. Mussolini's son in Ethiopia, bomb bursts like the flowering of roses. Flying Cobras or Loaches or Phantoms, or Jugs or SE–5s, for that matter, is the trip of trips. If they are bloodthirsty, it is impersonal; ten deaths, seventeen, are nothing more than a scorecard index of achievement and proficiency.

How then explain Wimpy's closing speech? A clumsy piece of Army public relations? A half-remembered line from some old Alan Ladd movie? Off we go into the wild blue yonder, down we dive spitting our death from under, only on the ground afterward we are really estimable citizens, ex-Cub Scouts to a man? Remorse for the dead and maimed back there on the trail? I doubt it, not from the boy who never talks when he's killing people.

(Although, in all fairness, the North Vietnamese are opponents sufficiently formidable to satisfy the most vainglorious fire-eater. Just last week a major from this outfit was gunshot by a heavy machine gun while flying a Loach, and in last year's Ashau campaign the unit suffered almost 100 per cent casualties.)

No, I think he was hinting at something less noble, more complex, more personal. He feels about flying as I do, at least a part of him does; it is, it can be, no, it *should* be, a precise occupation practiced in a pristine environment, dangerous at moments, challenging, exciting, all that, but the essence of its attraction is purity.

My last notation reads rather melodramatically and certainly not pro-phetically; think I will sell airplane when I get home. I would rather have had to shoot prisoners than participate in this afternoon.

Finally I went to bed, and, no great surprise, was kept awake by the frantic twitching of my mind. All the fine phrases I had written seemed evasions, cheap sophistries, tinsel rhetoric of the worst sort. There was a cold and persistent lumpiness in my chest. I felt as I had not since the age of eleven, when I shot a robin from our cherry tree with a BB gun. I broke its wing, but did not kill it, and knew I had to end its suffering. I shot it again and again, but it would not die, writhed on the driveway cinders chirping piteously until I smashed its head with the rifle butt. For months afterward I lay awake nights with this same feeling in my chest, fright and shame and sure knowledge that somewhere, somehow, there would come a reckoning in which what I had done would have terrible, if now nameless, consequences.

4

If flying in Vietnam revealed art as nightmare, even to so staunch a patron and practitioner as I, then it must also be said that very little about flying in the peaceful United States served to inspire.

Most of the laymen I knew regarded little airplanes as tinny, noisy, dangerous toys of the wealthy, accouterments in the class of yachts, and approached transit on the airlines with varying degrees of hostility. They saw aviation as one of those blights on the contemporary world akin to freeways and generating plants, a drain on the taxpayer, an assault on the acoustical balance of the environment, the keystone of military madness, an emblem of technology gone wrong.

A fair portion of those who traveled by air, who put the technology to their own use, considered the process a necessary dead time of express-ways to the airport, Muzak at waiting gates, security guards and potential friskings, bland-faced ticket agents and grown-up cheerleaders of steward-esses, a few martini and rubber chicken hours in an alloy cocoon. Journeys in sterility with undertones of queasiness. Airliners were perhaps indispen-sable ingredients in our life, quick and efficient, but in passage by jet any sense of flying, or of adventure shared, was as lost as Amelia Earhart.

And within the profession itself a majority had been transformed into unsympathetic types, self-righteous and self-justifying, venal, avaricious. Whatever the causes, you seldom met people who were in the game because they could not help themselves, who thought of themselves as artisans first and businessmen second, who were slaves to Lindbergh's wild freedom.

For example, at most auto filling stations in New Mexico the gross net profit on a gallon of fuel was five cents, seven at the most. Many airports in the area made a minimum of seventeen. I asked several operators about this, but their answers rang with all the sincerity and credibility of an East Village pusher explaining hard times to a hopeless junkie.

Or contemplate an item of maintenance, which might be called anything but atypical. The brains at Cessna decided to incorporate Ford inside-door handles into several of their models. The pieces, manufactured by Ford, were identical and interchangeable even to the stock numbers and the FOMOCO insignia stamped on their backs. At auto parts stores they cost less than $1.50, but Cessna Service Centers listed them for more than $6. I found one for sale at a Cessna dealer's for $14.33.

52 Labor in repair shops was expensive, which was all right if you got your money's worth, for no one but an utter fool stints on the care of an airplane, but the attitude and all too often the aptitude of mechanics were enough to enrage the most temperate owner. During the course of

one year I had an engine go rough in a serious situation because it had been timed incorrectly; a cowl nearly came loose in flight because it had been improperly secured; a landing gear jammed down when it should have retracted because the motor had been hooked up backward. At a shop where I had been spending an average of $300 for many months, an arrogant young foreman wanted to charge me $10.75 an hour for the use of an idle spray gun, 2¢ worth of solvent, and a mill of electricity. Another time I asked a mechanic I had considered a friend to help me cowl the big yellow bird, a job about as difficult and time consuming as moving a desk chair ten feet, and he said, "Not without a work order."

Too many pilots, who above all others ought still to be partial to the old mystique, were just as insensitive. Take an acquaintance, a charter pilot who was expert on modern milk stool tri-gears, machines every bit as exciting and distinctive as last year's Chevy economy sedan. He was a decent fellow, good beer company, kind to friends in distress, something of a rustic wit. One day we were discussing the merits of the big yellow bird. In an unseemly excess of enthusiasm I pointed out her superiority in nearly every regimen of performance to the newest and most expensive single engine products, went so far as to suggest he might well employ one in the charter business. He looked at me with an expression of genuine outrage tinged with pity. "The Staggerwing's nothing but a . . . a masculinity symbol," he said. "They may have been good planes once, but no customer would even want to ride in one today."

Lindbergh, almost alone among those who left written records of aviation's adolescence, had premonitions about its development and maturation. In *The Spirit of St. Louis* he alludes to a hint of unease, the desire on the one hand for aviation to grow, to prove itself, to justify its practitioners, link cities and continents and surpass nineteenth-century man's most extravagant science fiction fantasies, and on the other fear of a crowded sky, loss of the freedom and peace that are near the core of the aviator's art, tiny doubts, almost unrecognized and quickly suppressed, about the purpose of it all. Many years after his flight, when some of the worst of his forebodings were reality, he wrote in the preface to his remarkable book that ". . . we find ourselves moving in a vicious circle, where the machine, which depended on modern man for its invention, has made modern man dependent on its constant improvement for his security . . . even his life. We begin to wonder how rocket speeds and atomic powers will affect the naked body, mind, and spirit, which, in the last analysis, measure the true value of all human effort. We have come face to face with the essential problem of how to use man's creations for the benefit of man himself . . . "

Or, viewed from my less grand perspective, airplanes and pilots and mechanics had come to suffer from the same sclerosis as almost everything else in America: they had become computerized and regimented and regulated and organized, standardized and automated, mass-produced, agency-advertised, engineered for consumer appeal and easy handling instead of performance, made dependent on gadgetry in the name of efficiency and safety, but at the expense of initiative and craft. If aviation had once, for perhaps two decades after World War I, been analogous to Mark Twain's steamboat — the magical liberating fusion point of technology and spirit, the flame where promise of adventure and freedom were annealed with progress, in the good sense of that word — a complex and probably inevitable process had rendered it a business like any other, no better, no more rewarding, and just as subject to pettiness and stultification.

This was a state of affairs I sensed only dimly at first and chose to ignore

54

whenever possible. There was a challenge in mastering even the modern trainers on which I began, planes designed to allow the many to achieve minimal competence rather than to encourage artistry in a few, and a satisfaction in learning the dislocated dabs of practical science necessary to pass the government written, and I was lucky in my draw of instructors, was taught by two men who knew and appreciated the old ways and had maintained a pure luminous enthusiasm.

But I was even luckier in the circumstances of my journeyman's curriculum. I had been living in Mexico for several years before I learned to fly, and afterward, for two more years and several summers, I flew almost exclusively in that country. I do not think for a minute that either Mexican society or ethical atmosphere was inherently conducive to the preservation of the idea of flying as Lindbergh and others conceived it. Mexican rules and aviation officials, in the rare instances when I had anything to do with them, were even more cloying than their American counterparts. But poverty had retarded the pace of development, had kept officials scarce and regulations irrelevant, and the acutely rural nature of much of the country nurtured possibilities that were long forgotten north of the Rio Grande.

I took delivery of my first airplane in Dallas. It was a tiny and common Cessna with chattering brakes and nearly worn-out engine, a dowdy machine of shiny seats and much chipped paint — the only one I could both fly and afford. I flew home to Santa Fe for the weekend and then, with forty-nine hours in my log, nine more than the bare minimum for a private license, which in itself should be nothing more than a permit to fly in good weather with much caution, I headed south for Ciudad Juárez and points beyond, cocky and brash and proud and happy as a kid barnstormer in a newly surplus Jenny, the whole sky to explore, not so different really

55

from Lindbergh in 1923 when he barnstormed Mississippi with the earliest mixture of élan and timidity.

On the other side of the border I learned my Cessna thoroughly, flew it nearly every spare hour of every day, and began to instruct others. I also made the acquaintance of perhaps a dozen other types of aircraft, did a little Ag flying, taught myself the rudiments of instrument work, and explored a hundred isolated and usually uncharted strips from the Sierra Madres to both coasts. I traded the Cessna on a Citbaria, which was both a tail-wheel ship and strong enough to withstand aerobatics. I once flew five hundred hours over a six-month period without turning a radio on (there was no one to talk to, nor any station to navigate on), saw my first ice, exquisite and harmless traceries on the leading edges and windshield that time, and landed on a beach and dove for oysters and slung my hammock between coco palms. I got caught on top of an undercast, and flew for hours at the absolute ceiling of the plane, and flew into mountain waves (I had read of the phenomenon in textbooks), and made my first night-landing on a dirt strip but feebly illuminated by the lights of a pickup. The Citabria gave way to a four placer, and I chartered for rich Texans and flew at fourteen thousand feet without oxygen in order to put my passengers to sleep and circled ruins and cathedrals at wing-span height for photographers. I gave rides to burro drivers and dropped parachutists and retaught aerobatics to a World War II fighter pilot and put on amateur airshows at country fiestas.

I finally had to move home, for many and various reasons, but I never regretted an hour of my time in Mexico. It was an old-fashioned aeronautical education, almost impossible to come by any more, of dubious practical value in this age, but it served to make me aware of how things had changed at the norm. One part in particular stands out in memory as an object lesson in might-have-beens, or ought-to-bes, a felicitous wedding of commerce and exhilaration. It was a piece of flying I entered into casually, almost accidentally, with no more profound ambition than to gain a little unusual experience handling working airplanes in difficult circumstances.

It is early morning, six-thirty or seven, on the flight line of the airport in Uruapan in the state of Michoacan. Uruapan is to my mind a marvelous place, easily my favorite in Mexico. The town itself is heavy stone masonry, colonial bulk and substance which suggest a long and romantic history, red-tile roofs overhanging steeply pitched streets, a pine-lined boulevard, a park of surpassing beauty and a quick, pure white water, mountain river.

On three sides it is encased by the Sierra Madre Occidental, mountains worthy in altitude and majesty of the remotest Rockies, but swaddled in a mad mixture of vegetations: forests of high pine raddled with palms; myriad volcanic craters, from the outside piles of bare and hostile tufa, but with corn fields or lemon groves sheltered in the bowls; stretches of *altiplano* covered with wheatlike grass and patches of marijuana. It is as if you had mated Wyoming and Panama.

The airfield is a happy blend of utility and quirkiness. It is of adequate dimension, long enough to accept a fully loaded DC–3, and paved, but it also undulates like the track bed of an amusement park ride, a trait that causes the uninitiated to perform fabulous gyrations when attempting to land. The final course to the southwest runway is above a long and precipitous mountain slope. The approach is an extended glide perhaps fifty feet above the tops of the pines. You slide down for what seems like an hour, the power all the way back, the hiss of slipstream dominating

57

engine idle; the runway is foreshortened, looks almost wider than it is long; you sail past a yellow two-story building at the level of the upper windows (it is a whorehouse, called the Hotel Mexico, and I always think of Uruapan as the town with the girls at the end of the runway) and across the numbers.

But I come here not only for the scenery and because I find the place amusing. The field is home to several excellent mechanics and the most interesting bush operation I know. This morning the Barcenas brothers, David and Enrique, master mechanics both, are pulling an inspection on my airplane, and Salvador Rivera has invited me to fly down to the coast with him to share his day.

Salvador's airplane is a Cessna 180, a tail-wheel ship, demanding during ground handling, but blessed with superior prop clearance. It is an obsolescent type, scorned in the States by all but a handful of purists, even though it is noted for its ability to handle minuscule strips with enormous overloads and for its reliability and ruggedness. Salva once hooked the wing of this specimen in a tree during a takeoff from a beach strip. He was seventy miles from the nearest road, more than a hundred from the nearest mechanic, so he spliced the broken front spar with a coconut log and bailing wire, pop-riveted some roofing metal over the crushed leading edge, and flew home to Uruapan. The wing flapped a bit, but lifted willingly.

A walk around hints at a history of tricky labors survived. The paint is faded from many tropical suns. Here and there fresh patches of bare aluminum glitter like tinsel decorations. The leading edges of the prop and gear legs and horizontal stabilizer manifest the scars of collision with thrown gravel. One of the wings is dented from a bird strike. The interior is bare, stripped of all upholstery, soundproofing, and back seats. The floor is a much gouged and stained piece of plywood.

Salva's ground crew is cramming the baggage and back seat area with a wondrous jumble of objects: a case of Coca-Cola, sacks of feed cake, six-packs of beer, a case of two stroke motor oil, a packet of cosmetics, gunny sacks bulging with rice, flashlight batteries, a plowshare, boxes of ammunition. Each item is weighed carefully, not because anyone is very worried about overloading — we will fly with whatever we can shut the doors around — but because Salva charges by the kilo.

Last come the people, two men with gigantic sombreros, horny toes poking from splintering huaraches, belted machetes of formidable length, and a young woman. Between the pilots' seats Salvador places an elderly and ample matron in black. The landing gear is bowed with the weight. The tires look underinflated. The fuselage bulges from the pressure of elbows and knees. I remember that this airplane was designed for four people and hand luggage. A sporting man might give good odds that it is now incapable of becoming airborne.

We shut the cabin doors and find our movements severely restricted by the bulk of the matron. I can move my right arm, Salva his left. I pump the throttle for prime, turn on the magnetos; he trips the master switch and punches the starter. As we taxi out I imagine I can hear the gear groaning in protest. We Alphonse and Gaston our way through the run up, prop cycle and magneto check, and I half-hope to discover some fault that will prohibit flight. I lean the mixture. Airport elevation here is above 5000 feet. Salva reaches between the old lady's legs to set the flap bar for 20 degrees, then crosses himself, a gesture to the deities of ignition and oil pressure.

Takeoff is a prolonged and dreamlike affair. A moderately loaded 180 gains the air after only the briefest of ground runs and climbs with gusto, but we consume an unhealthy length of runway before I can feel our weight begin to shift tentatively from wheels to wings. I am working the throttle,

59

find myself pushing it against the firewall with more than a little vigor in hope of coaxing every last horsepower into the play.

Finally the upside of a dip catapults us skyward a few feet. Salva holds us aloft with his fingertips as the airspeed creeps up the dial toward safety. When the needle grudgingly touches ninety, he mines between the lady's limbs again and gently retracts the flaps. My face is covered with sweat and he smiles at me.

We fly southwest above the river gorge, the only direction not blocked by high Sierras. The terrain drops sharply and opens out into a wide agricultural valley, but 40 miles ahead of us are more mountains, the coastal range. Salva levels off at 5000, and turns on our one radio — an ADF receiver — for music. It does not work.

Salva flies with what seems to be graceful inattention. He holds the control wheel between the extreme tips of thumb and forefinger, as if it were a delicate but familiar piece of china to be handled with drawing-room daintiness. His eyes are hidden behind nearly opaque Raybans, an inevitable badge of the profession, and his upper lip is adorned with the merest dark shading of mustache. He wears a short-sleeved sport shirt and pale blue pants, both carefully pressed, and his shoes are polished to a high luster. The whole ensemble is quite incongruous with the airplane.

I have known him for some time, learned of his work in pieces and snatches, but we have never flown together before. He has a flair for hangar tales, most of which turn out to be outrageous understatements of his exploits, and he is embarrassingly generous. He sells me fuel at cost, often tops a tank for nothing, and a man would have to be far quicker of hand and eye than I am to beat him to a bar bill. Except for foot and mule travel, he is the sole means of supply and communication for a hundred-mile stretch of mountain and coastline. His little one-pilot airline combines the functions of pony express and freighter and ambulance and taxi for perhaps 2000 clients in mining camps and copra plantations and fishing villages.

We pass over Apatzingan, which is the crop-duster capital of Mexico, a town of forty thousand ringed with no fewer than five airfields. One is absolutely unique: a power line, marked by a tatter of cloth, neatly bisects the runway, so that any takeoff or landing roll must cross not ten feet beneath certain incineration. From our vantage we watch gaggles of Ag planes executing their graceful misty passes up and down the fields of avocado and chili and cantaloupe and honeydew.

Then, abruptly, we are in the foothills of the coastal range, all irrigation and greenery left behind. The 180 bumps and lurches in thermals. The peaks are up to 5000 feet higher than we, but Salva disdains extra altitude, points our nose for a narrow pass. A liter of fuel expended in unnecessary climb is a peso lost. The country is barren and uninhabited and nearly impassable: steep canyons, boulders, precariously angled outcroppings of bare rock, cactus, solitary trees stunted by lack of water and soil and twisted by winds, animal trails snaking through thorn bushes, an occasional abandoned hunter's hut lonely and crumbling on a ledge. It is impossible to imagine a successful forced landing.

Salva points out a mining strip on a hillside. The mine has been shut down for the better part of a decade, but when it was operating he flew in several times a week.

"How long is the strip?" I yell across the old lady.

"About two hundred and fifty meters."

61

I calculate that into feet, less than a thousand, which is right at the plane's minimum requirement lightly loaded. I know Salva was not going in and out of there lightly loaded.

We bank through the pass, wings dusting boulders, and ahead, at the limit of sight, the bleached heated blue of sky merges with the denser deeper blue of the Pacific. More rain falls on the seaward side of the mountains and some of the canyon bottoms have trickles of water and neat terraced little fields.

The major cash crops here are marijuana and opium. One spring I was flying this route on my way up from a camping trip on the coast and the country looked as if it had been subjected to a freak storm, for dozens of small sheltered places were powdered pure white. Closer inspection revealed not snow but clumps of gaudy opium poppies in full bloom. Salva told me later that the smell of them carries for miles, also that I was lucky no one had shot at me.

Our first stop this morning is San Pedro, a little dirt farming community set in the U of a box canyon several miles inland. The strip is strictly a one-way affair, and any miscalculation of the approach will cause our flight to terminate with finality against the canyon wall. Another hazard is livestock on the runway. A boy is stationed at the strip all day to keep it clear, but he has been known to sleep heavily.

I flatten myself against my door and Salva pushes the old lady into my lap. Even he will need two hands to make this landing. He reduces power, extends the flaps. We drop beneath the canyon rim in a long parabolic curve. A herd of goats on my side scatters. The strip is out of sight around a bend. Our airspeed has payed off alarmingly, and we are very low. One of my instructors used to say, "Altitude and airspeed are safety. When you're out of both, you're usually dead." Salva is employing quite a bit of power, has us hanging on the prop.

He is intent, even rapt, the corners of his mouth arched in the faintest of smiles. The old lady in my lap yawns. I am prey to a curious and

62

familiar sensation, a quickening of pulse, a narrowing of concentration, a detached curiosity. It is as if I am suddenly possessed of the gift to break time down, to examine even a moment at leisure and as it happens. I am not afraid. It is fascinating to participate in something and to be outside it too, and I want to know how it will turn out in the end, much as you might be curious about the final disposition of bodies at a good mystery movie. I would feel the same way were I flying the approach myself.

We round the final twist. The strip is dead ahead of us and at about our level. The boy is not asleep, is shooing a pig off the threshold. The 180 is at minimum speed. The stall warner honks like a startled gander. Aileron response is slow. Salva saws the wheel and jockeys the throttle. I can see now that the strip is canted uphill, which will help brake us, but it is also pretty rough.

Boy and sow pass under the wing on my side. The canyon wall is rushing at us. We touch, almost three point, and simultaneously Salva shoves the wheel full forward, which rocks us up on the mains for better braking and kills any lift the wings might be trying to exert, and retracts the flaps fully, and begins to feather the brakes. We tilt from side to side alarmingly in ruts and rocks, and I have time to hope we don't wipe the gear out. Salva brakes heavily for a few moments and the roll is under complete control. At the very top of the strip he pivots us sideways so the plane will not roll away, and cuts the mixture. A textbook, short-field landing on a field so bad and short any textbook would counsel to leave it alone.

Our reception committee is large, women in calico and a horde of small boys who follow Salva around and men armed with machetes and rifles. The people have skin the color of polished copper and features that are unusually angular, straight noses, strong chins, prominent cheekbones.

Local legend has it that the last Aztecs fled here after the conquest. Many are surprisingly affluent, beneficiaries of the drug trade, and others wetback into California or Texas every other year, come home with stakes that permit them to live in comparative luxury.

A jeep truck bounces up. It belongs to the town priest and is the only motor vehicle for seventy miles in any direction. It came here by sea, was landed across the surf on a raft, and the villagers cut a one-time road up from the beach. The road has long since washed out and the jeep is confined to hauling cargo to and from town over a half mile of ruts.

Salva dispenses mail and boards three hunters. We take off and fly downhill to the coast, set up an approach for another canyon strip, this one at the edge of the sea. It is sandy and even shorter than San Pedro. We approach down the canyon in order to land into the sea breeze. We round a last bend, skip over a mole and across a creek. The runway is lined with high brush, and a tree grows off to the left only a few feet beyond the reach of our wingtip. A horse materializes, ambles across the touch-down zone. Salva holds steady. Another horse. He swears, comes in with full power as a third animal trots between our main wheels.

We climb out over the water and turn back up the canyon for another try. The hunters are laughing. This time the strip is clear. We touch and I feel our wheels sink; deep sand grabs at them, tries to pitch us onto the prop, and stops us easily before the barrier of rocks at the end.

And so on through the day. We land at a little coastal town called Caleta where the runway begins on the lip of a cliff two hundred feet above wild surf and ends in a hillside; service two beach strips, long enough but very rough and made difficult by a strong cross wind; lunch at a copra plantation called La Tupetina. At Tupetina Salva refuels from rusty two-gallon tins he has cached in a shed, strains the gasoline with a chamois.

64

While the plantation siestas through the acetylene scorch of early afternoon, we bathe in a river. It is high-country cool — it runs underground to within a mile of the coast — and we dry off sitting on the roots of a giant laurel tree and smoke Vera Cruz cheroots. Salvador says, "Now you know my life."

We fire up, fly back to San Pedro, then down to yet another beach strip. At each stop people give Salva mail and orders for store goods from Uruapan. Several times we fly down the beach with our gear nearly in the foam. Once we pass two men on mules. They are entirely naked except for hats, and they carry shotguns slung across their shoulders.

On to Caleta again, the last stop of the day. This time we are greeted by the most famous citizen of the coast. He is an old general, a veteran of the revolutions, who boasts of fifty wives and three times as many children scattered among the villages and plantations. By his own account, he is nearing the age of one hundred and has only one last unfulfilled ambition, to sleep with an American hippie. He comes to the field to chat with Salva, to gather news from the outside and to comment on it, because he has heard there is a gringo on board.

We load a crate of langostina, fresh caught and still wriggling, and an old man and a woman with a sick child. The child has skin like tortilla dough and breathes rapidly in shallow snatches. He is too tired and hot and sick to cry.

Salva tells me to fly. I run the ship up to full throttle against the brakes. This is a short field practice of dubious technical value — some pilots contend that the cavitation of the propeller more than cancels out any advantage of starting the takeoff with the engine exerting its maximum power — but the noise and rattling vibrations lend me confidence. I release the brakes and we bump and jounce down the strip and over the edge of the cliff.

The sensation of sea underneath is sudden and a little startling, no matter that it is expected.

I make a shallow climbing turn across the water and take up a course for the pass. Great battlements of black and silver cumulus rest on the tops of the peaks, shoulder against each other angrily for air space. The sea is silver green and wrinkled. The sick child is asleep, cradled in his mother's arms. Salva draws deeply on a cigarette and rests his head against the side window. His eyes are closed.

I pick out La Tupetina and the hunter's strip and San Pedro canyon, revel in the whole wild sweep of the coast, surf and ocher beach sand and black cliff, coco palm and cove, palapa settlements, isolations of intense green, iridescent and strong as vitriol, in the canyon mouths, and jumbled mountain sides of gray rock and gray brown desert thorn. Automatically I monitor cylinder head and oil temperatures, adjust the controls against thermals, calculate the development of the clouds ahead, fiddle with the trim. The engine pulls strongly, and the needles of the instruments relay uniform messages of security and good health. The vibrations and noises are regular and soothing. I am completely satisfied, at ease, my pilot's appreciation of vista and the mechanical order of things garnished by a sense of usefulness and purpose.

During the course of several years I flew with Salva again many times. He acquired a second 180, and a Piper Super Cub, and on occasion I flew trips for him. He seemed to trust my piloting completely, which I took as the highest aeronautical compliment ever paid me.

I also came to know him fairly well. He was a solitary man, nearly an aesthete, for all his conviviality and generosity and his public role on the coast. He grew up poor near Uruapan and learned his trade the hardest of ways — boy plane-washer to mechanic to pilot. He told me he often went without eating for a few days to help pay for an extra lesson. His first ship was a 65 horsepower Taylorcraft, a dope and fabric butterfly runabout. In it he had all of his money and dreams, and his first engine failure as well. He got down in a jungle clearing in the state of Guerrero, near Acapulco, with only a bent prop. He walked out, got a new prop and parts, repaired the Taylorcraft and flew home.

He was unmarried, which was unusual to the point of uniqueness for a Mexican of his income and age (mid-thirties). Sometimes he imported a young coastal girl for a few months as housekeeper and companion, and once or twice his after-work drinking assumed serious proportions, and he took vain pleasure in his car, a new Volkswagen, which his ground crew was obliged to wash and wax daily.

But mostly he lived flying. He was aloft twice as many hours a year as the law would permit a professional pilot in the United States, and much of his time on the ground was spent working on his machines, overseeing routine maintenance and devising ingenious improvements, such as a new brake system, to make them more reliable. Even his conversation never strayed far from the true center of his attention. Any subject, no matter how abstruse or seemingly unrelated or commonplace, eventually furnished an opportunity for further discourse on his obsession.

After I had moved home, especially then, I found his operation was the one by which I judged others for economy and necessity and grace. The swept fin twins and awkward immaculate singles that appealed to the American flying public seemed to me not nearly so efficient or versatile or even beautiful as his honest work machines, and the transport of politicians and uranium moguls and bureaucrats and skiers was frivolous in comparison. Also, I took considerable satisfaction in the knowledge that he would no more entrust one of his runs to the average Yankee charter pilot, accustomed to long paved runways and tricycle gear and moderate loads, than he would deliberately fly into the side of a mountain.

But even Salva's future was limited, his operation tainted by the unmistakable forerunners of progress and growth. I visited Uruapan whenever I had the time and could afford to, and the changes were constant, manifest, and sad. The authorities closed down the old airport in favor of a new one boasting a runway of skating-rink smoothness and a terminal of poured concrete and plate glass, and year by year roads encroached on the heart of the coastal country. A dirt track reached Caleta one spring, was widened the next, and the government unveiled plans for a paved thoroughfare from Manzanillo to Zihuatanejo. The government also took to patrolling the opium and marijuana fields with helicopters furnished by the United States, which did not much diminish production, but did foster an atmosphere of suspicion and an intricate system of kickbacks, as well as considerable violence. Government patrols were armed with the latest American weapons and an obsolete M–2 carbine in firing condition was worth $500 cash to the natives. Salva said of the helicopter pilots that he fully expected their asses to look like Swiss cheese.

Salva, of course, was acutely aware of these portents. "They won't need me much longer," he would say. But he made no special plans for the future, would not consider modifying his operation to carry tourists, provide service from resort to resort. Sometimes, after a long day and a few rum and Cokes, when he was feeling melancholy and poetic, he would say, "It doesn't matter what they do, as long as they leave me some sky." It was a remark like many I had made myself, but we both knew it to be a plea, and a forlorn and wistful boast.

5

One flawless morning in the deep of winter I fired up the Staggerwing and flew from Espanola, New Mexico, to Pueblo, Colorado. I intended the trip as more than a passage between the two towns, a simple movement of some 180 miles with a transversal of La Veta Pass. It was to be an intellectual synthesis, an emotional catharsis, the capstone of much research and numberless hours of thought. The flying time was an hour even, but the journey was really backward in time toward certain truths I had been groping for and now wanted to see in substantial form. The catalytic agent in all of this was of course an airplane, a singularly special one, the last Vultee V–1A.

Vultee is a company known to very few people. Details of its history inspire no young businessmen, and the models it produced, except for the V–1A and a World War II basic trainer called the BT–13, which survives in some quantity, are long extinct. The organization was born in Los Angeles in the Depression, flourished briefly during the mid-thirties, was dealt a crippling blow by the Civil Aeronautics Board, and struggled on only to be swallowed and digested during World War II in a labyrinth of corporate contortions. All that remains of it is the V in Convair, the beleaguered division of General Dynamics which produced the F–111 swingwing fighter, also known as McNamara's Folly. Otherwise the name is as lost as so many others — Stinson, Waco, Fleet, Pitcairn, Ryan, Curtiss-Wright, Stearman. . .

Most of the original spirits are dead. Gerald Vultee, the founder and himself an amateur pilot, was killed with his wife in a weather accident near Sedona, Arizona, in 1938. I have a number of photos of him, all a bit yellowed and curling at the edges, a small, slight figure clad in the standard uniform of an engineer-executive of the day, banker ties and wool suits with wide lapels and baggy, cuffed trousers. They must have been quite uncomfortable in southern California. He had a high forehead and short wiry hair. In the photos his right eye is invariably screwed nearly shut, whether in objection to the sun or natural expression I cannot tell, but it gives him an aspect of unusual intensity befitting a man who had visions.

Dick Palmer, who was an engineer in the beginning, later a vice president, and one of the most gifted designers in the history of aviation, is still alive, but he has been out of the business for decades. A widower, he resides on a precipitous hillside in Whittier, California, in the company of an evil-tempered schnauzer. The energy and inspiration and meticulous intelligence which designed one of the first practical retractable landing-gear systems (on the Lockheed Altair and Orion series) and the world's fastest landplane (for Howard Hughes, a single-engine, one-place, low-wing monoplane, to my mind the most esthetically pleasing ship ever conceived) are now devoted to his garden, a botanist's delight of citrus fruit trees and unusual palms from several continents and orchids and rare flora. Its boundaries are a chain-link fence, which the schnauzer patrols aggressively several times a day, towing his master behind. The house has a terrace at one side and the view from it must once have been remarkable, a handsome vista encompassing Long Beach and downtown Los Angeles, a panorama of the heartland of promise and progress, but these days it is limited more often than not to the pines lining a boulevard at the base of the hill. "The smog is pretty bad," Dick wrote recently. "If I were younger I'd leave, but it's too late for that now."

Dugal Blue, another of the engineers, and my uncle Tom Van Stone, the stress analyst and test pilot, were killed in the crash of an attack bomber prototype in 1935. Other specimens of this ship were built, but never with much commercial or military success, and the last is thirty years in a fiery grave, so my uncle's legacy came to me not as the prize exhibit of a museum or even a chapter in the history of famous airplanes, but in one medium-size briefcase with sprung hinges. Envelopes full of dusty photographs of old racers and military biplanes, brittle newspapers with banner headlines blaring flame and catastrophe, a manila folder bulging with sympathy letters, a list in my mother's hand of people to be thanked for flowers, and a small box containing naval insignia, ornately carved gold buttons and gold wings. Forlorn trinkets.

Yet my uncle is an undeniable force in my life, a figure of irregular but legendary proportion, real as any living relative, a model and a specter. Neither my mother nor grandmother, while she was still alive, could speak of him at length, though my mother was quick enough to invoke him when I quarreled with my younger brother. "He never picked on me," she would say. "Why can't you be that way with Jimmy?" Our house has a long portal in front made cool in the summer by a veil of lace vines, and suspended from the beams midway along it was a green swing of no great artistic merit but extremely sturdy construction. My uncle had carpentered the swing, and I knew from an early age that it was supposed to be unique. I was in my mid-twenties when my mother retired it, without explanation, and I was slightly shocked. My grandmother used to tell, smiling a mother's pleasure and wonder forty years after the event, how Tom had picked her up "as if I didn't weigh anything at all" and carried her the length of the portal when he came home after his first year at college. But mostly he was not mentioned, his death a tragedy so vivid and dark any contemplation of it was best avoided. Naturally he has always fascinated me.

His boyhood, as nearly as I am able to reconstruct it, was smalltown, narrow, happy, busy, tinted with Horatio Alger ethics and yearnings. Almost from the first he displayed an unusual equilibrium, a sense of what was right, of where duty lay, that did not make him either pompous or self-conscious. "He was gentle," my mother says. "He could take care of himself, but he never bore malice toward anyone." I have one snapshot of him at about age ten. He is wearing plus fours, a wide tie, and stiff collar for the camera; his hair is parted in the middle and he is skinny, almost frail. His chin has a pronounced cleft, which is something of a family mark. He is standing beside my mother, a robust and dimpled child, nearly as tall as he, more substantial, and he is looking at her with an expression that is at once protective and bemused, as if he knew his responsibility as her guardian but also her redoubtable strength of will and hard intelligence.

74

He was always an achiever, and his record reads like the wholesome fiction some press aide might fabricate for an ambitious politician. He was an acolyte in the Episcopal Church, and he had a paper route, and he had his share of small boy adventures. A clipping from the Santa Fe *New Mexican* dated November 9, 1914, tells that he was "badly bruised last night when he rode a bicycle full tilt into a rope stretched across the street at Catron Corner, where paving is under way. The rope caught the boy under the chin and threw him heavily to the ground. There was no lantern on the blockade."

He liked the outdoors, used to go camping up Santa Fe canyon behind the town with friends, or my mother, and a pack burro, and he hiked alone into the Sangre de Cristos, sometimes as far as what is now the Pecos Wilderness area, long lung-searing taste of new pennies in your mouth climbs into the true high country, remote and vast and not much changed since the mountain men, since Kit Carson; there were beaver streams and flash of native trout and boulders bleached white as fine linen and pebble-bottom eddies glittering kaleidoscope colors and wind in the long-needled ponderosa and scrub oak and then quaking aspen and peaks of granite stabbing above timberline like accusing fingers and little lakes so high that even in midsummer skim ice formed at night, sudden-startled mule deer and turkey and bear tracks, air pure as first snow and alpine meadows, wild flowers nodding in shoulder-high grass, and quick thunderstorms that cleansed each afternoon. You turned an unexpected corner on a trail and could look behind you at almost the whole of north-central New Mexico, a world rimmed by mountain ranges, its topography as salient as a bas-relief. You could look across fifty miles to the soft blue silhouettes of the Jemez, or south seventy-five miles to the Sandias, north across the Taos Plain into Colorado. Five thousand feet below was Santa Fe, adobes merging into

75

piñon hills in nearly perfect camouflage, a town more at ease with its surroundings than any other, a good place to start from and a better one to return to. West from town the hills sloped down to the dark wound of the Rio Grande gorge, sun glint winked off the narrow gauge tracks of the Denver and Rio Grande Western, the Chili Line, at Buckman Crossing, and between the river and the Sandias were the volcanic fire-polished black stripe of La Bajada and a middle distance expanse of overgrazed brown tinder Indian flatlands called the Domingo Plain. It was an enormous sweep that became to Tom something more than the sum of its mileages and the intimations of its place names, became a sort of key to his consciousness. The distances and vistas, the long spaces, the big sky, the perspectives and perceptions were much like flying, and they drew him again and again. Usually he went there alone.

But it would be wrong to picture him a loner, an estranged and poetic young man seeking solace in solitude, for in fact he was something of a joiner, and one of those people who attract contemporaries, to whom teachers attribute the qualities of leadership. He was an Eagle Scout and an athlete, holder of the state record for the mile-run in high school. Senior year he was also captain of both football (the field was gravel-covered and his knees were scabby all fall) and basketball, president of his class (twelve students), and valedictorian.

For college he chose Harvard, which was a certified gateway to the sophisticated, competitive East, a logical next challenge. The choice is further explained if you consider the family in the context of those days. We were members of whatever social elite the town had, friends of judges and senators and the wealthy, but we were also, so my mother is fond of reminding the blessed of a later generation, very very poor, and Harvard must have seemed the key to familial solvency.

76

My grandfather was a man of strong convictions, which he took pleasure in expressing forcefully. (A Bull Mooser, he was elected to the state's first corporation commission. He detested Woodrow Wilson as the epitome of vacillation for his Mexican policies. He had three roosters, a blustery but spineless one called William Jennings Bryan, a scraggly, cowardly one which hid behind the hens and was called Wilson, and a handsome strutter of a Rhode Island red, a rooster's rooster, which was naturally called T. R. My grandfather liked to walk with friends around the chicken yard discoursing on politics using the roosters as props. My mother describes him as "lovable," but when I have done something she considers incontinent or rash she is apt to say, "You remind me of my father." Once she told me, "He was always writing letters to the editor.") He died just after World War I and left very little more than the house, which was mortgaged.

My mother baked all the bread herself, she and Tom sold eggs for pin money (the greatest debacle of their youth occurred when a dog slaughtered their whole flock, the political triumvirate included. Mother makes it clear the carnage was secondary to the financial loss), my grandmother was forced to sell part of the property to support Tom in Cambridge, he himself spent the summer before freshman year on a wheat gang in west Texas and rarely came home from school during vacations for lack of train fare.

There was no money at all for my mother's higher education, so she taught school in a little central New Mexico town where the chief industries were coal mining and bootlegging. (The period was marked by two nadirs. She had to deliver a neighbor's baby almost singlehandedly, and one of her suitors, unbeknown to her but not to the local populace, was a Prohibition agent.) My grandmother worked at the Museum of New Mexico, a job which encouraged her considerable talents in art appreciation, but was not very remunerative.

Tom clearly carried with him a multitude of collective hopes and expectations and subtle never-phrased responsibilities. The family's honor and reputation as well as its welfare must often have weighed heavily on him; its name was plainly his to make. He never displayed any talent for the financial, lived close to the bone, died broke, and was not ever in a position to send anything home. But in other areas he acquitted himself well.

He was modest, self-effacing almost to a fault, popular in adult life as he had been in high school, even cherished by his comrades. Among the letters of sympathy are several from pilots and engineers and fellow naval officers, awkward of phrase but clear in meaning — he was one of the rare ones, a talented pilot, a skillful engineer, the noblest of companions. He also disliked gossip (a note from Dick Palmer to my grandmother tells of a luncheon spoiled by a flyer from Tom's reserve squadron, who related a series of malicious rumors about officers at North Island Naval Air Station), drank well, had a sense of humor. In fact his only recorded flaw seems to have been in political prognostication. A letter from him in September 1932 expresses assurance that "Hoover will win again. I think he deserves a chance to continue through the tough period and try to carry out his ideas."

Even Harvard did not alter his personality or change his values much, and he was Class of 1925, there in the heyday of the Final Clubs, the height of the Jazz era when young men were supposed to feel beautiful and damned, the reign of that iron Brahmin, President Lowell. A man less smooth-tempered and secure would have been subdued or driven to become what he was not, perhaps destroyed. None of these things happened to Tom, but nevertheless the contrasts must have been deep cutting. He came from a town of eight thousand where the buildings were made of mud, three fourths of the population spoke Spanish instead of English, firewood was delivered by burro, and culture was delegated to a group of matrons (my great-grandmother was a founder) who called themselves, without any idea of connotation, the Women's Board of Trade. His clothes were of the wrong cut and cheap, he held four scholarships simultaneously and still had to work outside, and he thought Saint Mark's was a cathedral. In all, he must have been like a minor character from Marquand, a true friend of the protagonist, one of those eager and open outlanders, who, when brought home to Sunday dinner in Weston, ate with the correct fork but failed at small talk.

He was one of only five mechanical engineering majors in his class and an honor student, and those distinctions led to an offer of flight training in the Navy Reserve. He spent the nights of one semester in ground school at MIT and passed the physical, although he had been worried about his visual acuity. He had not yet come into his majority, so my grandmother had to sign a waiver before he could begin instruction in an actual airplane. She told me once she had had grave misgivings, but later, when she heard him talk about airplanes and flew with him (he took her up several times and once looped her), she knew she had done the right thing.

He flew first, for twenty-nine minutes, on 17 August 1925, in a type identified in his log as TG. It was undoubtedly a biplane of open cockpit design, probably it was a landplane, but I have been able to discover nothing more about it. His instructor was a lieutenant commander named Davis, who, after fifteen flights and twelve hours and forty-four minutes aloft, signed him off for solo.

That fall, after graduation and solo, he went to work for Westinghouse in Philadelphia as an engineer-salesman of commercial generators, a position of promise with a solid concern that almost guaranteed security, steady promotion, final affluence. Yet this appears to have been the only protracted period of loneliness and dissatisfaction in his life. He wrote home more frequently than at other times, requested the addresses of Santa Fe acquaintances, dwelled on good times with the Harvard friends he saw in passing. My mother remembers that he hated Westinghouse, was bored with generators, disliked Philadelphia, stayed on as long as he did only because he was in the habit of seeing things through.

His flying was confined to weekends and that was clearly at the root of his malaise. He had tasted the exhilaration, and the prospect of neat progressions up the corporate ladder was scant competition. The Navy offered a temporary way out, so in 1928 he requested and received a year of active duty. In August he ferried a Boeing fighter from Rockaway, Long Island, to North Island at San Diego, with an unauthorized stop in Santa Fe en route, and joined the *Saratoga* at sea. He had never made a carrier landing before.

During his months attached to the *Sara* she visited Panama and Japan. He brought home a few photos of Panama City, which even then was very Americanized, and many more of the surrounding jungle that fascinated him. From Japan he brought kimonos of brocaded silk for my mother and grandmother, and two bottles of duty-free *Dans la Nuit* perfume. (My mother has her bottle yet.) His logs are filled with gunnery practice, target tows, section tactics, dive bombing practice, and fleet tactical maneuvers. I have snapshots of him with friends, standing formally in dress whites, serious and handsome and self-conscious of the camera, and lying in shorts on an overside crash net taking the sun (he is tousle-headed and still skinny); and dozens more of the airplanes, a lover's record of affection, all types from every possible angle, in the dim hangars below deck, ready for launch, at touch down with the arrester hooks trailing, tangled in crash barriers, being manhandled by deck crews, and a series of one going over the edge. When the year was up there was no question of returning to Philadelphia or Westinghouse.

He lived alone for a while in an apartment in Glendale, then rented a house in Burbank, on Orange Street, with Dick Palmer and Dugal Blue. Tom wrote home that "we have a beautiful view of the San Fernando Valley. There are great big windows in the side of a large living room . . . and a nice fireplace opposite. Dick Palmer, the Cal Tech boy, plays the piano very well and has a piano here. Duke Blue is fond of music also, contributing records of Ravel and Muossorgsky for our Victor. I can add nothing but my little radio."

Dick Palmer wrote of that time, "Tom had more friends than any man I have ever known . . . I would bring around young ladies whom I considered very swell, and after meeting him they would pump me for all the information they could get about him. This greatly irritated me at first, but I soon became used to it." Often I like to imagine the two of them — I have no clear impression of Duke Blue — the pilot and the piano player, the dashing airman and the austere engineer. Of course it was not that simple; Dick had a pilot's license, Tom could work on a slide rule better than the next man. But Dick was shy, the most reserved of men, and Tom attracted people, and always there was the bond of the airplanes.

Tom worked first for the E. M. Smith Company doing structural analysis and test flying on a midwing sport plane and in 1931 moved to Vultee. (Gerald Vultee had succeeded Jack Northrop, the mind behind both the Vega and the DC–3, as chief engineer at Lockheed, and designed the Sirius, in which Lindberg and Anne Morrow explored the Orient for Pan American, before striking off on his own. His intention was to manufacture a memorable transport, all metal, retractable gear, much faster and more

81

economical and comfortable than the Ford and Fokker trimotors which still dominated airline flying.) Tom liked the company from the first. He was logging plenty of time in advanced machinery and was beginning to be known as a coming engineer, and the planes quickly established an excellent reputation: no early Vultee was ever faulted by a pilot for lack of performance or strength.

A girl friend, Janet McHendrie, wrote, "He had more fun than anyone I know. He was doing the thing he loved, working hard on airplanes, and he loved hard work and he loved planes. No one disliked him. His men friends and associates literally worshiped him, and at least three girls in Los Angeles were sitting around waiting for him to telephone . . . He was so real and so natural that he was all tangled up in our lives . . . "

The approach to Pueblo is interesting. The big yellow bird and I cross La Veta at 11,500 feet, turn the corner of high mountains, and 40 miles ahead a gray industrial smudge oozes out on the pristine snow of the plains. Pueblo approach control frequency is clotted with voices, a variety of little planes and two United Boeing jetliners, down from the United training base in Denver to practice landings.

The visibility lessens as we descend, penetrate the dome of pollution. I strain ahead for the airport, reduce the airspeed and glance frequently at the map. I dislike landing at airports like this. For years near most cities in the East navigation on even the best of days has been made annoying by the effluent in the air, but now cities in the Southwest, where visibility was formerly restricted by the limits of sight or mountain ranges, are coated by increasingly dense layers of scum. I suspect that within my flying lifetime the atmosphere over the entire country, perhaps the entire world, will be so foul as to make instrument flight mandatory at all times.

Approach hands me off to tower. I still do not have the airport in sight,

82

though I know from the map it cannot be five miles away. "Left traffic two five left," the tower says. "United Boeing jet on right base two five right." I spot United, a 727, then the airport. Gear down, flaps, roll onto final. A quick scan of the ramp beside the runway, but I do not see the Vultee. Attention back to the task at hand.

The yellow bird touches and rolls out. Fifty yards to the right United does the same. I turn her off toward the terminal, go to ground control.

"Where's the Vultee?" I ask.

"In the hangar to your right."

A lineboy beckons me into a tie-down slot. I shut the Pratt down, searching the hangar as I do. It is cavernous, filled with planes, including a couple of medium modern twins. However, one whole rear corner of it bulges with a ship utterly unlike the rest — broad curved expanses of bare aluminum, an endless wing of graceful taper, a single great radial engine attached to a mighty three-bladed Hamilton Standard, flat-sided windscreen canted in a unique reverse rake. She dwarfs all the others, a condor caged among sparrows.

Harold Johnston, the man who owns the Vultee, meets me on the ramp. We shake hands, stand awkwardly. He has never seen me before. I am not sure where to begin.

"Well," I say. "There she is."

"There she is."

I spend an hour inspecting her, running fingertips over her satiny aluminum skin, pressing rivets, peering into wheel wells, examining her 1000 horsepower Wright Cyclone (Harold has wiped off every trace of oil and I am embarrassed for the Staggerwing, whose cowl is coated with the stuff), trying to assimilate her vastness. By contemporary airliner measurement, of course, she is not outsized, but in the context of small planes, even top-of-the-line executive twins, she is immense. Her tires are huge and smooth and bulbous, black doughnuts for a giant; her wingspan is almost double that of my Beech; her fuselage is a tremendous tapering cylinder with room inside for eight passengers and two pilot seats, a lavatory, luggage compartment, radio compartment.

Harold has appointed her cabin with much care and taste. The chairs are covered with leather, the walls with wood paneling and rich fabric. I sit in the cockpit. The ceiling is low, the windscreen close by my cheek. The control levers are mounted on a central pedestal, like a big multi-engine ship; they are large, substantial as the controls of a cat or a steam shovel, and worn shiny from use. The wheels are wood, look like fittings from a yacht. After a few minutes the care and logic of the placement of every element in the cockpit becomes apparent. Each control and switch is stationed in a convenient spot. You could fly this ship under the most trying instrument conditions and not have to twist your head away from the essential dials. My hand moves easily and naturally to throttle, mixture, elevator and rudder trim, gear and flap controls. Vultee and Tom and Dick Palmer and Duke Blue did their job well from a pilot's stand-point.

I ask Harold the innumerable questions I have stored up, and often they lead him into fascinating asides. He is a small man, bespectacled, jaunty, in his forties, a Texan by birth, auto mechanic by profession; once he was a crop duster. Occasionally he is profane, frequently very funny.

The Vultee came into his life almost a decade ago when a man towed her up to his garage behind a truck, her wings removed, and wanted to rent the space in back to park her. Harold asked why he didn't park her at an airport but the answer was evasive. "Turned out later he didn't want to put her at the airport because he had about a dozen people he owed money following him around and they wouldn't think to look for her at my place."

For two years she sat. The man never paid any rent; children bombarded her with rocks. Finally Harold arranged a sheriff's sale and she was awarded to him. "Thought maybe I could break even on the rent if I sold her. I didn't think about rebuilding her." Two men from Ohio came with the intention of making her airworthy enough to ferry home. After two months they were destitute and Harold repurchased her for less than they had paid him. "I thought maybe I could just keep selling her," he says. "Seemed like I had a good thing going."

The airplane was a shambles. The instruments were smashed; the windows were broken out; the cabin was piled with miscellaneous unlabeled parts, some of which didn't even belong to the ship; the fabric control surfaces were punctured and rotting; no one could guess what wounds time and inactivity and dirt had inflicted on the engine. Harold kept looking at her and thinking that no one in his right mind could conceive of her as anything but a candidate for a recycling plant, and yet she nagged at him day after day, something about her lines, clean and strong, intimations of what she had been, what she had represented, the places she'd flown, the people she'd carried. His wife asked, with apprehension, if he was thinking of restoring her himself. "I haven't decided yet," he told her. "You'll be the first to know when I do."

He built a shed around her to hide her from passers-by, protect her from further assaults by malicious boys. "I got to thinking she must have come to me for a reason," he says. He made the fateful announcement to his wife over breakfast one morning, but she was not surprised. "The job took five years. Five years working sixteen hours a day. Still, she was in amazing good shape, considering. They built her to last."

He had no formal training in engineering, had never even attended college, but machinery had been his life, and he was not awed. "Hell," he says. "I figure an engine is an engine." He hired a licensed aircraft mechanic to help him, but the man was overwhelmed by the magnitude of the task and didn't stay long. "No matter," Harold says. "Shortly I knew more about her than anybody else anyway." Remember that the Wright brothers themselves were only inspired bicycle mechanics.

There were no plans to refer to, no engineering data to be consulted, no warehouses with spare parts, not even any fellow owners to provide moral support. The FAA was skeptical at first, then helpful, but still Harold had to struggle through bales of paperwork. He replaced everything he even suspected had been attacked by corrosion, some seven hundred square feet of metal in all, using old parts as templates for the new ones. She was an unusually stout ship, stressed for twelve positive and four negative Gs, partly thanks to an underskin of corrugated aluminum. Harold had to design his own dies to reproduce it. He found a faulty gear in the engine, but no replacement was available at any price, so he had the metal analyzed and fabricated one himself.

His business suffered, to say nothing of his family. "It got so bad my own dog didn't even know me. He'd bark like hell when I came home nights." He was a member in good standing of the Pueblo Chamber of Commerce, mentioned at one meeting he was thinking of naming the ship the *Spirit of Pueblo*. Some thirty of his colleagues visited his shop, looked at the bird, her wings off, her interior bare, and suggested that this wasn't exactly the sort of advertising the city needed.

He took the fuselage and engine into the dirt alley beside his garage, fired up the Wright. The glass was still broken out of the windshield and the prop blast was almost blinding. The instruments were makeshift. He had run her for perhaps fifteen minutes when he noticed a police car beside him, lights flashing angrily, though he couldn't hear the siren over the thunder. The prop had thrown a solid jet of dust across a main thoroughfare half a block away and traffic was backed up. A crowd of several dozen had congregated. "They just wasn't used to thousand horsepower cyclones," Harold says.

When it came time to move her to the airport he discovered she was too long and far too wide to qualify for a trailer permit, but a sympathetic highway department official waived regulations. Harold had been away from piloting for a long time, had never flown anything of this magnitude, and a retired Air Force officer with many hours on a variety of machines volunteered to handle the test hops. "I was with him, of course. We were supposed to be doing taxi tests, but he just took her off." She flew perfectly, although both men were preoccupied with the landing ahead. "He come in way too hot," Harold says. "I could feel it. He used up nearly the whole runway. This ship don't need more than a goat field." He did the rest of the test flying himself, which proceeded without serious problem.

Since he has piloted her to several antique fly-ins, where invariably she wins all the top trophies available, and on numerous business and pleasure trips. She has a range of nearly 1500 miles with good reserve, a ceiling of 30,000 feet, and will operate with enthusiasm off the most marginal strips with a payload of over a ton. Once, going into Houston, Harold passed a pressurized twin worth a quarter of a million dollars, the ultimate state of the art-business machine, with "about fifty knots to spare." He has a desk full of newspaper and magazine articles about him and the Vultee. He went ahead and named her the *Spirit of Pueblo*, and the chamber of commerce was delighted.

87

He began to fill in the blanks in the history of the type; he found old pilots who had flown them, and mechanics who had worked on them, has accumulated over six hours of tape recordings of their recollections. There were only twenty-five built, his is serial number Twenty-Five. Number One flew in February 1932 and Tom's log for that month notes weight and balance checks, and fuel consumption tests, demonstrations to American and Pan American. They set a number of intercity speed records (two hours and fifty-nine minutes from Chicago to New York in 1935). Jimmy Doolittle broke the transcontinental record in one, and another, wings filled with Ping-Pong balls for possible flotation, held the transatlantic record. They were also direct competition for several types of great renown, the DC–2, DC–3, and Boeing 247. In many ways they were superior craft; they carried almost as many people about fifty miles an hour faster at barely half the operating cost. But in 1936 the Civil Aeronautics Board forbade the lines to fly them at night or in instrument conditions, which severely limited their utility on the routes. The rationale was lack of two-engine safety, though their accident record was as good as any of their competitors.

The *Spirit of Pueblo* belonged initially to William Randolph Hearst, Sr., and was his second Vultee. (Tom checked out Hearst's own pilots.) She was based at San Simeon until 1939 when she was farmed off to a Panamanian named Tito Gallaberet, in whose service she pioneered many routes in Central America and was almost demolished when she hit a U.S. Army dump truck while landing in the Canal Zone the day after Pearl Harbor (no one was hurt). The army bought her from Gallaberet, repaired her, and sent her to the embassy in Bogotá to ferry dignitaries around South America.

By the late forties she was back in private hands and based in Panama and Costa Rica, flying for Hollywood jungle movies, hauling monkeys to the University of California Medical School for research. You can imagine her then, a haughty old clipper finishing out her days in the island trade, proud still with remembrance of times past. Her belly is tacky with oil, a flaked paint scheme blurs her lines, the skin behind her exhaust stacks is burnished, her prop blades are gouged by gravel and the debris of primitive strips, her ground crew is composed of Latino empiricists, geniuses of baling wire and the monkey wrench, and her pilots are rugged men, any cargo across any sky, throwbacks to tramp captains from Conrad's day.

For decades she plied the grubby secondary routes, Central America and the Caribbean and Mexico, and paid the inevitable price. Corrosion here, a little unattended electrical problem there, a belly landing in Mexico. Finally she came home, punchy as an old club fighter who years ago lost track of what round, out of license, with squawk sheets measured by the yard, still flyable but only barely. She crossed over at Brownsville on the mouth of the Rio Grande and gathered herself for one last long effort, flew up across Texas and into Colorado to La Junta, owned by an entrepreneur of dubious means who promised restoration but delivered the odyssey of dismantlements and cross-country truckings and unpaid bills at many repair stations that finished behind Harold's garage.

Again Harold says, "There must be some reason she ended up with me."

The first time I visited Harold, the Vultee had a mechanical problem which prohibited flight, but three weeks later I am back in Pueblo on a fine afternoon, faint breath of spring in the air, and she sits ready in front of her hangar. Harold apologizes that she is not polished, but to me she is perfect; the sun glints off the long spread of her wings and the centerpost of her cockpit windshield leans forward eagerly.

We climb in, along with two flight students of mine and two local friends of Harold's. He shuts the cabin door and we clamber up past the passengers into the cockpit. The first order of business is to open the side windows and reach around with a cloth to wipe speckles of oil from the front of the windscreen. Harold adjusts fuel valve and battery switch, works the wobble pump for fuel pressure, trips in the inertia starter. A long rising whine. When it reaches peak frequency he flips the starter switch to mesh, the prop blades jerk quickly past. The cyclone catches, belches blue oil smoke and settles down to a muted thunder with undertones of clatter. A glance out the side window reveals a fence lined with spectators. The ship vibrates steadily.

Taxi visibility is much better than in my Staggerwing, and she responds nicely to applications of brake and rudder. Pueblo is beset by the usual hordes of traffic, a stream of light planes and another pair of United Boeings. We rumble past a modern retractable single, and the pilot gapes. I wave nonchalantly. Harold performs the ritual of mag check and prop cycle and I bask in the noises and throbs.

"Pueblo Tower," Harold says. "Vultee Zero Nine Nine ready."

"Vultee Zero Nine Nine cleared for takeoff. What is your direction of flight?"

"Oh, north," Harold says. Direction is unimportant, what matters is that we're going.

We line up down the center of the runway. Out the window I watch a United 727 lower its landing gear on the downwind leg. Harold advances the throttle, slowly and smoothly, even tenderly. He has labored over this engine too many hours to abuse it. We vault forward, Harold raises the tail almost immediately. In seconds we are flying, climbing steeply at an airspeed that would sustain no other four-ton machine but a helicopter.

Harold works the gear switch, and the wheels start up, pulled by an

90

electric motor far superior to my Staggerwing's. Our earphones reverberate with the shrieks of its labor. The red gear-up light blinks on. Harold signals me to take over.

I bank gingerly away to the north, lower the nose for greater airspeed. She feels solid and steady as Gibraltar, but she isn't mine, and I'll be damned if I want the distinction of stalling her at 700 feet. With 55 per cent power she is climbing more than 500 feet a minute. At 7500 I level her off, trim the nose down. She accelerates and then accelerates some more. Soon our airspeed is more than 200 miles an hour. If we had time or reason we could climb to 15,000 where she could make 250.

A few exercises reveal her to be both mannerly and responsive. Hands off she has no inclination to wander from course or altitude, roll into a turn and add a twist of trim and she slides around as if tracking a rail, but the gentlest nudge on the elevators brings an instant change in pitch.

"What do you want to do?" I shout at Harold.

"Anything you want."

I can think of a hundred things. I'd like to put on the oxygen and climb until we could see the earth curve away into Chihuahua and the sparse air outside would be cold enough to stick my hand to metal and then wing over and run down the long delirious burning blue to skim across the Colorado snow fields and pull up again in an arcing zoom until the nose locked on the sun; I'd like to fly her a thousand hours, ten thousand, slip onto a beach strip I know in the state of Colima in Mexico, at dusk, with the long Pacific rollers on one side and palms on the other, and climb her through fog into the brilliance of morning and slice through a fall night in New Mexico with starshine on the wings and the radios turned down so all you could hear was the engine rumble and the strong hiss of the slipstream; I'd like to take her back to southern California, land

91

at the airport in Van Nuys where Tom used to fly, so Dick Palmer could see her, look at her against a backdrop of modern planes and know how well she's stood the harshest tests of time; there's no end to things I'd like to do, the places I'd like to go, the people I'd like to see. But Harold is paying for this and even throttled down the cyclone burns forty gallons an hour, so I do a few more turns, lock on headings and study her instruments and then shout to Harold, with the greatest reluctance, "Well, maybe we ought to go back."

"O.K., I'll show you how she lands."

He calls Pueblo Tower, which sequences us behind one of the United behemoths, and slides down to pattern altitude. He flies a leisurely approach, turns onto final maybe three miles out. The gear comes down with more wailing in our headsets. He pulls on a dab of carburetor heat, trims the nose up. We are doing less than a hundred indicated. He has told me how well she handles at low speeds, but still I feel an involuntary tensing: big heavy airplanes are supposed to land fast. Over the threshold, black stains of burnt rubber skim beneath. I dare not look at the airspeed indicator, but still she transmits no signs of stalling, not even a burble. The wheels touch, our speed seems no faster than a crawl. Harold comes back in with the power and we are flying again.

"You shoot one," he says.

"You're sure?" I keep thinking she is the last of her kind, not mine to break.

"Sure," he says.

I level off on downwind, trim, make positive that my hand knows the power lever from the mixture. Harold sits with his arms crossed, an imitation of a man relaxing. United is ahead of us again. An optical illusion makes it seem that we are catching him. I am sorely tempted to call out for everyone on the frequency to hear, "Hey, United. Hurry up, there's a real airliner behind you."

I turn base, trying to approximate Harold's path. A glance into the cabin behind. Our passengers have been following developments with a keen interest, know that I am in control, and I detect more than a hint of apprehension in their expressions. I am not worried in the least. I ought to be, but am not. She feels so familiar.

"We'll make this full stop," Harold yells.

"O.K."

Harold lowers the gear. Green light comes on, three hanging. I work the trim, feed in a touch of power to compensate for the increased drag. She rolls onto final, the long concrete stretches ahead. Harold extends the flaps. Again I work the trim. Ease back on the power, the engine note changes, the airflow hiss subsides a point, we start to sink. The unlit neon ladder of approach lights is under us, a red plumb line to the threshold. Back a little more on the power, up a shade on the nose. I am not checking the airspeed, there is no need. She is talking to me, telling me what to do. It is as if we have done this together many times before. I want to laugh and shout. Now concrete slips under wings and wheels. I let her down the last few inches, the tires kiss with a tiny squeak. I bring the power all the way back and we roll out. Finally the tail comes down. My only thought is to do it again and again and again.

Late at night, long after my wife is asleep, I sit in my workroom looking at photographs. The desk and table and filing cabinet top are strewn with them. I hold in front of me one taken of Gerry Vultee and Tom, shortly before he was killed. They are standing beside the attack bomber, which is a modification of the V–1A, greenhouse in place of the cabin, bomb-bay door in the belly, and machine-gun ports in the wings. Tom has just completed the final Department of Commerce certification flight, and Vultee wears an expression of exaltation combined with relief. He looks a bit like the father of new twins.

Tom is calmer. He is noticeably older than in the Navy pictures, wiser, less exuberant. Strong lines crease his forehead and the corners of his eyes are furrowed in the way of old pilots, workman's scars borne in testimony of many hours spent close to the sun. The eyes themselves are brown and set very deep, like my own. He wears a vest, quiet tie; his pockets sprout pencils. Veins stand forth clearly on the backs of his hands.

I look at the picture and think over my flight in the V–1A and wonder what he would think of her now, think of me flying her, of all that has happened. I wonder if he would look with approval on those 727's United was flying around, for they are really only logical extrapolations of the machines he built, the current products of forces he helped set in motion. Somehow I think not.

He and the others were visionaries who for all their imagination and inventiveness never foresaw more than a portion of what would transpire. He was as different in temperament and personality from me as a man could be — yet I suspect he would appreciate my kind of flying and my kind of friends, the mechanics with whom I am congenial, the pilots I admire.

Most of them are considered cranks and romanticists by the charitable, no-goods and crazies by others. All of them find it onerous when working within aviation's mainstream. They are men like Harvey McGuire, a gimp-legged mechanic-pilot who rigged a bubble machine on an open cockpit 1928 Curtiss bathtub pusher, hired a hardy young man to sit shirtless

94

in front scrubbing himself with a long-handled brush, and flew over a Los Angeles freeway at rush hour, trailing fantastic streamers of soap balloons. The idea was to sell a shampoo, but the result was a nine-hour traffic jam, and wreckers were hauling off the automotive debris for days. Or Jim Franklin, a young acrobatic pilot, who flies a Waco biplane around the eastern New Mexico plains inverted and about five feet off the grama grass. Or Fred Duran, master mechanic, hangar philosopher, a connoisseur of fine machinery with great brown eyes sad and soft as a bereaved setter and a rake's flourish of a Mexican moustache. He once dissuaded me from selling the Staggerwing during an expensive maintenance crisis by saying, "She's like the most beautiful whore in the world. Drive you up the wall seven ways to Sunday, but in bed you forgive her everything." Or Manuel Duran, Fred's brother, war hero, pilot and engine man, who can tell you from memory the valve settings on a Wright Whirlwind, but often forgets his own telephone number. Or Salva. And Harry Bodenner, who spent several years of a long career ferrying junk airplanes and says fondly of that time, "I had so many forced landings I quit looking for good fields and picked the ones near telephones." Or Harold Johnston himself. In another time and place he might easily have been a Montgolfier or Glenn Curtiss.

Only partly in jest I call such men the true believers and I have not met many of them. They hold not so much to the old ways as to what the old ways stood for. They have no common denominator of age or background or class or physical type, but a certain sense about the possibilities of flight, what it ought to be and what it usually is not. In forming their judgments, which are mostly intuitive and rarely articulated, they have, of course, the advantage of much hindsight.

I look again at Tom. Within the hour the bomber's cyclone will fail

95

on takeoff and he will face the hardest of final decisions: straight ahead into houses full of wives and children, or a turn made with insufficient altitude and airspeed back toward the field. True to character, he will opt for the field, and perish when the ship stalls into high tension lines.

There is not the faintest hint of nervous foreshadowing in his expression, no premonitions, just the image of an engineer and a pilot, a man taking a moment for posterity from the work he knows and trusts. He is calm and professional, at peace, sure not of what life ought to bestow, but of who he is.

6

Under various conditions, then, flight can be beauty and peace and provide insight into the patterns of human affairs, both personal and public, but it is first and last, and probably most important, a vehicle for self-discovery, a means to test your skill and knowledge and resolution against adversity. That is an aspect much down played by professionals, who out of congenital modesty will tell you there are old pilots, and bold pilots, but none who are both; and the manufacturers, who insist that flying may be learned rapidly and adequately by nearly anyone who can drive a car; and the FAA, which would have you believe that thanks to the thoroughness and wisdom of its rules, the splendid accuracy of the science of meteorology, and the reliability of modern machinery (all licensed to intricate government specifications) any flight that leaves the ground with proper preparation will be secure and serene.

Perhaps, but listen again to Lindbergh. "Can that be why so many pilots lose their lives? Is man encroaching on a forbidden realm? Is aviation dangerous because the sky was never meant for him?" Or discussing the Atlantic crossing: "If I make the whole flight without meeting anything worse than those scattered squalls over Nova Scotia, I'll feel as though I'd been cheating, as though I hadn't earned success, as though the evil spirits of the sky had disdained to sally forth in battle. A victory given stands pale beside a victory won. A pilot has the right to choose his battlefield — that is the strategy of flight. But once that battlefield is attained, conflict should be welcomed, not avoided. If the pilot fears to test his skill with the elements, he has chosen the wrong profession."

Battlefields, forbidden realms, a celestial malignancy to be challenged and conquered. Hardly. Flying is safe, really and truly. I myself have been known to deliver a half-hour lecture to doubting passengers, replete with quotations from actuarial statistics, to prove that travel in a good light plane, properly maintained and competently piloted, is the safest means of transport devised by man. And yet . . .

One time instructing in a Cessna the rudder came unhinged. I had checked the bolts myself that morning, so had two of my students. Had the elevator gone instead of the rudder I would have died for sure.

An acquaintance, a pilot of enviable reputation, ran into his own rotor wash in a helicopter. The machine was destroyed, the pilot shaken up considerably, the passenger seriously injured.

Another acquaintance, a professional, hit a hilltop five miles from an airport he had been using for years, spent months in the hospital, emerged in a framework of braces. His eyes were set in the bright vacant glaze

I remembered from certain young marines in Vietnam, the men stationed in the heavily shelled firebases below the DMZ.

In Vietnam, a helicopter flying formation not a hundred yards from a ship in which I was riding exploded for no apparent reason. Three friends dead.

Another professional, a man whose aeronautical beginnings dated back more than forty years to Standards and Swallows and Eagle-rocks, to Hissos and OX–5s, Liberty DHs and Sunday crowds at county fairs, was run down and killed by an air force jet not ten miles from the Albuquerque airport. Both planes were in radar contact.

A charter pilot of several decades' experience hit a hilltop on a night approach in Nevada and died.

An airline pilot, a wise and gentle man, a true believer with whom I practiced aerobatics in small planes, crashed into houses near Midway in Chicago during an instrument approach. All crew and passengers were killed. A film taken moments after impact shows my friend trying to struggle from the cockpit window. He never made it and died of burns and smoke inhalation. The route was one he had been flying for fifteen years with a record of perfect safety.

A duster pilot, a friend in Mexico, crashed on takeoff. The plane caught fire and he was incinerated while twenty people watched helpless. Some said he had collided with an especially vicious dust devil. Not five minutes before I had drunk a Coke with him, helped him choose a ticket for the national lottery, and taken off myself in the big yellow bird.

All these friends and acquaintances damaged or destroyed within a span of two years, and none of them were neophytes, innocents, only half-trained or plagued by poor equipment. Proof enough that progress and technology, science and commerce, have not had much success in shackling the evil spirits; reminders of the penalty for failure, evitable or otherwise, in aeronautical tourneys.

Every so often, no matter what your degree of experience or type of aircraft, you have a flight that pushes you to the limits of your resources, stands you face to face with the difficult, and forces you to contemplate the truths of possible disaster. Such flights are not the norm, but they stud the logs of any serious pilot with a random consistency. Let me describe just one. It was not a record attempt in an untried craft, was in no way a tribute to some special talent of mine, for any number of more experienced men would have considered it a drafty and cold piece of routine, but for me at my level there was enough of the unexpected and the unknown to extend the boundaries of my abilities and cause me anxiety and a glimpse of fear. And when it was over, a trace of pride in victory honestly won.

It began on a cold gray November afternoon at a strip in the heart of the Texas rice belt, near a little elm-tree town called Cuero. The ceiling is low, visibility is no more than a mile. I am walking around my new mount, an open cockpit Stearman biplane, a type of mean reputation. They were built in the early forties as military trainers, and wags said, "There are two kinds of pilots. Those who have ground looped a Stearman, and those who will." The beast sits high on rangy legs, and the main gear is placed far forward, none of which promises easy handling. And this particular specimen is no resurrected primary training playtoy, but a crop duster, in which role her original Continental 220 has been replaced by a gargantuan 1340 Pratt and Whitney of 600 horsepower. It is comparable to dropping a blown Indy Offenhauser in a battered jeep.

102

I am to ferry her to Las Vegas, New Mexico, and her former owner, a wise old Ag pilot and charter member True Believer, has left me a note of much wit and equal foreboding. It reads in part: "Tom.

She is a nice flying old bird. I have checked her out. But be careful.
1) Be careful on the brakes or you will end up on your back. 2) Be careful
with the throttle or you will end up on your back. Good luck. Henry."
Dusters work on short strips and this Stearman has been re-equipped with
truck brakes powerful enough to halt a locomotive, ten times over powerful
enough to catapult a plane onto its back if improperly applied. The 600
horsepower, if not handled on a gentle rein, will accomplish the same.
I can receive no check out, a few comforting introductory circuits with
someone ready to retrieve my mistakes, because the front seat and dual
controls have been removed to make room for a hopper. It occurs to me
that Henry is not here himself because he can't bear to watch.

I climb in, clad in long underwear, regular clothes, lightweight flying
coveralls, winter flying coveralls, jacket, mittens over gloves, felt-lined boots,
my old motorcycle hard hat. I am close to suffocation, feel as though
I am working weights in a gym when I lift my arm. The 1340 Pratt sports
a 24 volt starter, but the plane has no integral electrical system. Hence
what little view I have over the nose is filled by hood-raised cars, connected
to each other and finally to the starter by dozens of yards of jumper cables.
A mechanic stands by with a fire extinguisher. Another is placed at the
starter, an arm's length behind the prop.

"Switch off."

"Switch off," I repeat.

He engages the starter and the prop grinds through several revolutions.

"Switch on. Brakes on."

"Switch and brakes." I make the magnetos hot.

"Contact," he says. The old litany.

The Pratt catches with a report like a field piece and a cannonball of
black smoke booms out of the stack, whizzes down the fuselage past my

ear. The mechanics disengage the umbilical jumpers, the cars back away carefully from the lethal medallion of propeller. The Stearman is alive with the vibrations of a mighty power, rocks alarmingly on her springy gear, and the Pratt is only idling. Jesus, I think, what will happen when I shoot a little throttle to her? I remember stories of World War II fighter planes, P–51s and Corsairs. If you went firewall on the power at low airspeeds you didn't have enough rudder to control the torque and the planes would roll on their backs against your every desire and effort. I doubt if either of those fighters had a better horsepower-to-pound ratio than this bird.

I study the gauges carefully. There aren't very many of them, as agricultural flying is strictly seat-of-the-pants. No flight instruments except altimeter and airspeed, so I will have to stay out of the clouds. A glance overhead, the ceiling is oppressively low. I consider shutting her down, saying I'll wait until tomorrow. Nonsense. I have flown in worse weather in lesser planes, and I have a very long way to go. I can still see and know that westward along my course the conditions are better. I motion the mechanics to pull the chocks.

Taxiing I begin to gain confidence. Her brakes are indeed quick, but they have good feel. Just remember to touch, not stomp. She has excellent tail-wheel steering, and I can get a fine forward view by leaning out the left side. I turn around at the end of the strip, run the engine up. If anything the vibrations are less with a little boost. Mag drop O.K. Carb heat works. Prop cycles fine. Oil pressure and temperature O.K. Set the altimeter. The hands are yellowed with age. Only the compass bothers me. It twitches through variations of thirty degrees. Probably no problem; it will settle down as the bird smooths out in flight.

The big moment. I tell myself, unconvincingly, for the hundredth time,

104

that she's just another airplane, with a prop and engine and stick and rudder and elevators like all the others; I line up ever so carefully down the centerline, feed in the throttle gently as a caress. Even so we leap forward, accelerating like a double A fuel dragster. I am ready with right rudder, but the bird has no excessive tendency to swing left. I raise the tail, still nothing abnormal. We are airborne. I note that the throttle is not halfway to the stop. What a machine!

A moment to sigh in relief, wave at the mechanics as they pass underneath, congratulate myself on still being alive. Then the problems start. I reach in one of the many pockets of my winter flying suit for my first map, but trying to unfold it in the manner I want is about as easy as typing on a motorcycle at speed. All my previous open cockpit flying was in areas I knew, where I needed no maps, and I had not counted on the eddy effects of a ninety-mile-an-hour wind compounded by prop blast. Finally I take the glove and mitten off my left hand. Instant frostbite, but I am able to force the paper into usable form.

Now where are we? Cuero has been swallowed up in the mist. I spot a rail line, one of several leading out of town. I check the compass to see if this one is laid in the right direction. Surprise. The compass is spinning like a top, a whirling blur of numbers. I cannot obtain even the most wildly approximate bearing from it. The altimeter is also playing games, is unwinding and presently informs me I am flying a thousand feet below sea level. But this compass is serious. East Texas is singularly featureless — I remember the panic of my first cross-country solo, conducted in the same area, when all roads looked alike and never ran exactly where the map said they should, but I had a radio in that plane and simply followed a signal back to San Antonio — and I have no idea which way I'm going. I could turn around, but that probably wouldn't help matters.

I decide to press on, as the runway was pretty well aligned with my course, and one railroad track was pretty well aligned with the runway. If I didn't turn while fiddling with the map I ought to be aimed in the general direction. Sooner or later the track will lead to something I can correlate with the map.

I relax a little, feel out the bird. She flies nicely but is none too stable. Take my hand off the stick and a wing drops. She is also slow, held back by a chemical and seed spreader affixed to her belly as well as the drag of massive gear legs and myriad flying wires. It is said of Stearmans that no matter how many horses you give them they still cruise at 90 mph. Which brings up another problem — range. The Stearman carries only 44 gallons of fuel, enough to feed this Pratt for no more than an hour and a half at moderate power settings, so any flight of more than 125 miles will bank on luck, favorable, or at least neutral winds, and perfect navigation, and here I am lost already. In fact I may have set a new record — lost two minutes after takeoff.

Ten minutes pass. Fifteen. The ceiling is lowering, and I am mildly alarmed. I know it was clear to the west, because I just flew in from there. It is getting colder too. I am down to telegraph-pole height, peering ahead alertly for landmarks. Also I search for towers — I am well below the top of an average radio tower. I had better find something pretty quick or else pick a landing ground. There is an abundance of fields, but they are all quite wet and I would chance nosing over. I can always use a farm road, but that is likely to incur the wrath of authorities. Still, the prospect amuses me. Set her down beside a farmhouse, stroll up to the kitchen door in my flying togs. "M'am, could you tell me which way to San Antone?"

Twenty minutes. Fear is beginning to constrict my chest. I do not like

106

this at all. In places the clouds merge with the crops. And the engine is throwing oil. All radials do to some extent and I know very well that a few drops spread along the windshield and fuselage by the knife of the wind are nothing to worry over, but the narrow screen ahead of me is absolutely opaque. If I stick my head out to see, my face and shield are pelted with hot droplets.

Then a few houses pass under my wing, a road joins the track. I try to match these events to a position on the map, and fail. A tower looms ahead, red warning lights blinking feebly. I break off to the left, give it wide berth in fear of guide wires. More houses, the edge of a town. Maybe I'm back in Cuero. I make for a water tower at no more than fifty feet. I can see tricycles and brick barbecue pits and lawn chairs in back yards. If some irate citizen takes the Stearman's registration number I will have a lot of explaining to do to the FAA. YORKTOWN it says on the tower. I never heard of Yorktown. I put the bird in a tight bank around the tower, search the map frantically. Christ. I swear aloud. Yorktown is south of Cuero. I have been headed toward Mexico, not the Rockies.

Twenty minutes later I am circling the airport at Cuero. Someone once said the moment of truth in a new airplane is the first time you have to land her. I line up on a long final, feel sweat oozing out of my armpits. The runway looks too short and cruelly narrow, though I know its dimensions to be more than adequate. There are fuel pumps to one side, and I think that if I do lose control I must employ any expedient to avoid hitting them. Over the trees and I chop the power. The bird drops like a disconnected elevator. Evidently 1340 Stearmans are not fond of gliding. Back in with some power. Ease into a flare. Wait. Seconds stretch into years. Precious runway flees beneath. Nose up a bit more. The tires squeak,

107

the Stearman rolls straight as a plumb line. It wasn't hard at all. Relief and a queer disappointment mingle.

One of the mechanics climbs up on the wing, alarm in his face. "What's the matter?" he shouts over the engine. "Don't she run good? Henry said she run fine."

"She runs all right, but the compass doesn't work. I got lost."

He peers in at the offending instrument, which is still spinning gaily.

"Hell," he says. "We never thought to check it. All our pilots know where they're going."

An hour later, I am refueled and airborne again. A fresh compass, ripped from another airplane, is attached by baling wire to the dash, where it works sensibly beside its insane relative. The engine is still throwing oil, but it has not missed a beat, and I have taken precautions to ensure visibility. Tucked beneath my new compass are rags and a bottle of Plexiglas cleaner, so I can wipe the windscreen and my face shield any time I need to. The events of earlier are confined to memory, stored for some unforeseen future use. Such happenings rarely frighten me in retrospect, instead foster what may well be a dangerous illusion, for I feel that each problem coped with, each emergency overcome, merely burnishes the armor of my experience against the next.

Which is not to claim bravery for myself. I am occasionally afraid in airplanes — this afternoon I nodded to fear and tomorrow morning I will shake hands with it — but since fear is one of the pilot's worst enemies, on a par with weather, an eroder of confidence and impairment to clear, precise thought, it is something I hope I have learned to force into the background, to ignore. I have tried to teach myself to consider it just another factor in my chosen element, a problem like fuel distance, or compass deviation, I can solve by the application of reason.

Rarely am I afraid of flying itself, as opposed to alarm or even gut terror at some circumstance peculiar to one flight, but that is a phenomenon much less easily dealt with. Such episodes occur unpredictably, perhaps twice a year, at four-in-the-morning moments when nightmare becomes insomnia, and I imagine the details of my demise with great if irrational vividness, my brain heated and blurry and out of control and a cold talon-fingered hand squeezing my intestines. The antidote is simple, a quick and guaranteed cure — fly as soon as possible the next day.

But now there is no reason to be other than pleased with everything. The sky ahead is clear. I am following the right railroad track, know exactly where I am and where I want to go. A road runs beside the track and the Stearman plays with cars. I am flying low, partly because it is warmer, but mainly because it is fun. Anyway crop dusters don't run well above a hundred feet. They're not used to it. A yellow Ford Mustang with a pretty girl in the right seat passes me with ease; I add some boost, the Pratt thunders, I lower the nose and pay off a few more feet for airspeed. We creep back abreast. The girl waves.

On our right is a large airport, an auxiliary field for Randolph Air Force Base, and a pair of needle nosed T–38 jet trainers are shooting touch and goes. They fly like white lances, slice through the air at incredible speed, even in landing configuration. I watch with interest but no envy. I have bummed rides in a couple of two-seat jet fighters and found the experience curiously sterile, automated, lacking in sensory joy. The instruments told fantastic stories, my cheeks and blood sank with Gs on a pull out after a bomb run, and the pilots were obviously able men, well trained and disciplined, but there was an air-conditioned antiseptic quality to those

109

flights, they were too high, too short, too fast, and I prefer it right where I am, with the wind in my face and flying wires at my shoulders, flying a machine that was obsolete in 1942, pulled along by an engine designed in 1925.

Daylight is fading and ahead is my destination airport, New Braunfels. We are not far from San Antonio, where I have friends, and I look forward with relish to describing the day's adventures. I circle the field once, note the windsock. It is an elaborate establishment, many concrete runways of great length and breadth, a number of modern machines parked on the ramp.

I land, taxi toward the tie-down area. Quite a crowd, at least five or ten people, is gathering to watch my approach. A man directs me into a slot and I chop the engine. People press up against the ship.

"Where you from?"

"Cuero."

"How long it take you?"

"About an hour." Cuero is almost exactly eighty-five miles away.

"Hot damn, she's a fast one, ain't she?"

"She's not made for speed," I say, a little defensively.

"How many horses?"

"Six hundred."

"Hot damn, that's a bundle."

"We heard you come over, and we all come outside. We thought you was Orville and Wilbur."

Beneath the banter I sense respect, perhaps a touch of envy.

"You gonna spend the night?"

"Yes," I say. "Fill her with eighty and let's put in a gallon of oil. The heaviest you have."

The man in charge is very nice, efficient and considerate, and in a few minutes the Stearman is ready for tomorrow and I am scrubbing at the first layers of oil and sweat, waiting for my friends. My face in the lavatory mirror is windburned a deep red brown and Lava soap is not about to remove the grime from the creases in my knuckles. I am beginning to look the part of an old-time airman, an observation which pleases me greatly.

Takeoff next day goes well. The airport attendant is philosophical about being rooted from bed at five in the morning — I have seven hundred miles to cover, so an early start is imperative — and only a little nervous at standing a few inches behind the prop to work the starter. The Pratt goes on the first try, breaks the still with its historic thunder, and as I taxi out, I give my best dawn patrol wave to the friend who has brought me to the field. That she is an extremely statuesque blond does nothing to detract from the scene.

Airborne, I get my map out, pick up my course, and begin to learn about the true meaning of the word cold. The morning wind has an Arctic cut, a thousand tricks to thwart the most extensive clothing. It sifts between layers until it reaches my skin with the consistency of ice granules. I pull every zipper to its limit, rewind my two scarves a dozen different ways, put my hands in my armpits, sit on them alternately, stamp my feet and kick hard at the tubular-frame members to help circulation — all to no avail. I think of the old barnstormers and air mail pilots with new wonder. The tortures of riding an open cockpit ship in the Midwest, say on Lindbergh's old run from Saint Louis to Chicago, at night in the dead of real winter defy imagination. Or the World War I fighter pilots, who took machines not so very different from this one as high as twenty thousand feet, to patrol and fight. At twenty grand the temperature is often many degrees below zero. Combat must have come as a welcome diversion.

For a half-hour everything is placid. I rumble over the lake country between San Antonio and Austin, watch my progress across the map. There is an overcast, but it looks thin, lets the sun show through in places in a low-wattage glow, and I have plenty of room to maneuver. Then, quickly, the overcast begins to thicken and lower. I pass above a ranch strip, debate about landing to wait for improvement. But I have miles to go, promises to keep, time is important — the Stearman is meant to be towing sailplanes at a soaring meet this hour tomorrow — and yesterday the Pratt showed a stubborn reluctance to start again after it had been running. Today I have made up my mind to replace fuel and oil without shutting down. I cross a highway that eventually leads to Johnson City and the clouds drop even lower, no trifling matter now, for we have left the flat lands behind and are winding between hills.

I feel the unpleasant familiar constriction in my chest. I am following a gravel farm road, flying a tunnel between cloud and hillside. I tell myself there is nothing to worry about, so long as there is room to turn around. But what if the clouds are dropping behind me in an impenetrable curtain? They shouldn't be — the weather forecast was favorable, this is mostly ground fog, a morning condition which usually dissipates rapidly with sun and heat — but I would happily trade a month's university salary for gyro instruments, for even a simple twenty-dollar, vacuum-driven turn and bank. Then I would not be helpless if the next turn reveals an impasse, and I am forced to begin my retreat blind.

Instrument flight without instruments holds a special terror for me. Once
112   I was practicing in a Link, an artificial training apparatus so realistic it is not at all uncommon to emerge from a session in one sure you have really been aloft in a storm instead of flying stationary and safe indoors, and the plane began to gyrate as if it were in a flat spin. Nothing I did brought it back under control. I shoved the nose down, added power,

chopped power, employed full opposite rudder and still the wild descent continued until there was nothing left to do but sit there with my stomach knotted in panic. Just before impact I came to my senses and climbed out, shut the machine off. The trouble was a blown fuse, but some corner of my mind refused to believe I wasn't dead and I walked around the room for several minutes touching things like desk chairs and paper clips with groveling humility. Spiraling into a Texas hillside with vertigo is definitely not the way I want to check out.

We pass a farm that looks like a leftover from *The Grapes of Wrath* — barn of bleached boards with sagging roof, sagging corrals, junked cars with rusted fenders sitting on blocks, a few scraggly cows with hip bones stretching their hides, a sad house with all its lines and angles driven askew by wind and years, a windmill so rusty I can almost hear it crank over the sounds of engine and slipstream. What a place to crash.

Another twist in the road and I can go no further. Clouds and earth are one. I add throttle, drop the left wings in a tight bank, feel the Gs shove me hard into the seat as the right wing cleaves into the overcast above. I concentrate on keeping the left lower tip on a gate beside the road, do not want to drift into a hill. We level out, fly back down the road and over the farm with my pulse pumping rapidly. A woman is standing in the front yard, wearing a long dull dress like a sharecropper's wife in a Walker Evans photograph. I wave but she does not return it, just wheels slowly to watch us pass. In a moment of fancy I imagine she might be Dame Death.

We pick up the black top, turn toward Johnson City. To follow this road will take us north of course, but it is better than turning back. Forty-five minutes have elapsed. The cork in the glass-tube fuel gauge ahead of me bobs at the halfway mark on its journey to empty.

The Stearman plays yesterday's game with cars, passes them ever so slowly, but my mind is elsewhere. Twice I follow openings to the northwest, am forced back by lack of visibility. On one try I press an instant too long and we are swallowed by a cloud. My turn is a desperation affair for I lose all but the barest contact with the ground to veils of mist. I am aware again of blood shoving through my arteries at unnatural speed.

Even on the road the clouds are too low for comfort and seem to be getting lower by the minute. I work ahead of the bird on the map to ascertain the location of towers, but never keep my eyes inside the cockpit for more than a few instants. It is wise not to trust maps totally. I remember once in Mexico, on a day only a little better than this one, I was following a rail line when it disappeared abruptly into an uncharted tunnel.

Ahead now a power line crosses the road where it drives between two hills. The wires are at my height, perhaps 75 feet, just below the murk. I slide into the middle of the road, the low point, and drop. If a car comes through that pass the driver will be in for a distinct surprise. We flick under the lines with a wing span to spare, our wheels brushing the pavement.

An hour and thirty minutes. The fuel cork is bottoming now, and some time ago I employed every trick I know to stretch the last gallons. I have leaned, though we are thousands of feet below where that is advisable, and set the prop to turn 1600 rpm, so slowly I can count the separate blades. But there are clusters of houses, the harbinger of towns, and in a minute I am over Johnson City, spot the airport, which turns at an angle to the main drag. I circle once, squirt Mirror Glaze on my face shield and wipe with the rag. No time to bother with the windscreen. I ease power back, slip over some high lines, flare, and hear the lovely squeak of rubber on asphalt.

The runway is pocked with chugholes and the field is deserted, home to not even a weekend pleasure craft. I taxi its length hoping to discover some sign of occupancy, climb out of the bird and chock her wheels without killing the Pratt, and run into the street. I feel like a man in a space suit, some television Martian invader. Drivers see me and cars swerve. My toes tingle with returning blood. I barge into the office of a heavy equipment company; a blocky man with mechanic's hands looks up from a desk.

"Help you?"

"I need gas." I am panting. "Landed at the field over there. About out of juice. Bird won't start when she's hot."

"There's a pump there," he says. "But the fuel ain't been used in a year. Contaminated for sure."

"What can I do?"

We hear the Pratt rumbling in the background. How many drops left?

"Well," he says, "tell you what we maybe can do."

Within ten minutes I am feeding auto gas from a Mobil pumper into the Stearman's tank. Several pick-up loads of spectators watch. She takes forty-two and a half gallons. I climb down, say to the Mobil man, "I thank you very much. What do I owe you?"

He thinks a minute. He is tall, sandy-haired, wears a droll expression. He looks at the bird — her fuselage sides are glistening with oil, the Pratt grumbles gratefully — and at me. "Nothin'," he says.

"No, I owe you. I really appreciate your coming out here."

"Hell, son," he says. "This time it's on the house. Flyin' a machine like that you need all the help you can get."

No one, least of all me, takes the line as humor.

The rest of the trip was eventful, perpetually interesting, even exciting, painfully cold, but never difficult. The clouds lifted a little and then burned

115

off. I indulged in the childish pleasure of flying over Lyndon Johnson's billion-dollar homestead on the Pedernales about ten feet off the rooftops with both prop and throttle at their forward stops. A man at a west Texas airport refused to sell me fuel unless I killed the engine — how he thought gasoline was going to blow forward against the hundred-mile-an-hour wind from the prop to ignite on hot cylinders escaped me — so I had another fretful twenty minutes watching the cork before the next town. At a stop in Santa Rosa, New Mexico, the Stearman landed in a twenty-mile-an-hour direct cross wind without a dicey moment. So much for the legends of groundloop.

And finally, after some ten hours of flying and refueling, I brought her home. The eastern sky was night and the Sangre de Cristos were a wonderful twilit purple, almost black, inky, a dark jigsaw bas-relief against the muted blues and streaky red of last sunset. There were no clouds, no wind. The landscape reposed in perfect calm. I felt flat and a little sad. I set up my last approach, fought through my fatigue and the cold to make it a good one, and touched and rolled out and taxied her to the hangar as they turned the runway lights on. I was weary to the last molecule of marrow, partially deafened by the constant tear of wind and heavy snoring from the Pratt; my face was permeated with oil to the bottom layer of epidermis; my ears were crimped into aching nubs by the helmet and I knew my legs and back would be stiff for days. I pulled the mixture to idle cut off, but as the rumble faded away and the Ham Standard spun on I had an almost irresistible urge to shove the mixture rich again, to catch her before she died and take off and climb for the evening star doing rolls and loops along the way.